The Wisdom of Oz

The Wisdom of Oz

Ruben Turienzo

LONDON   MADRID
NEW YORK   MEXICO CITY
BARCELONA   MONTERREY

Published by
LID Publishing Ltd.
6-8 Underwood Street
London N1 7JQ (United Kingdom)
Ph. +44 (0)20 7831 8883
info@lidpublishing.com
LIDPUBLISHING.COM

A member of BPR

businesspublishersroundtable.com

Printed in Great Britain by T J International Ltd.

ISBN: 978-1-907794-04-9
Collection editor: Jeanne Bracken
Translation: Don Topley
Cover design: Laura Pérez Reyes

First edition: June 2011

To Freckles, my inspiration.

Contents

Foreword

The Wisdom of Oz is a business book like no other. At a time when the words 'wisdom' and 'business' rarely inhabit the same sentence, Rubén Turienzo has written a business fable that excites and entertains the reader as much as it provides guidance with issues of personal effectiveness and success. Drawing on a classic, timeless story, Rubén Turienzo shows how to get people engaged and focused, how to inspire trust and create a winning team, how to be self-confident, and how to develop as a successful leader. Based on *The Wizard of Oz*, the story and characters are familiar and more relevant today than ever.

Sadly, the business world is often depicted as being cold, selfish, fixated on finance and utterly soulless. In the early years of the twenty-first century the reputation of business in general, and business leaders in particular, has never been lower. This portrayal, however, is only a small, distorted fraction of reality, and Rubén Turienzo shows us the other, larger part. Business is a noble enterprise and leadership is a courageous, exciting and fulfilling activity. The road to leadership and personal success may at times be tough, but it is always worthwhile and ultimately rewarding.

And if you don't believe me, just ask Dorothy. Dorothy's life-changing adventure begins when she joins the Oz Company, New York's largest and best-known advertising agency. There she learns the power of teamwork, the role of communication, the need for drive and determination, and she discovers the values and vital skills that will help bring her success.

Dorothy's journey to motivation and courage is one that will be instantly recognizable to many people around the world. Along the way, she encounters Miss Toto, Frank Wizard, Mrs East and Heidi North and other characters who either help or hinder her. With the characters and morals of *The Wizard of Oz* combined with the glamour and seduction of *The Devil Wears Prada*, Rubén Turienzo shows us that the challenges Dorothy faces are the ones we all face in our careers. These include: dealing with fear and uncertainty and finding inner strength, motivating and inspiring the people around us, doing the right thing, making the best decisions, overcoming challenges and making progress. Personal growth is the destination and this elegantly-written fable provides important lessons on how to take control of your life and career and move forward.

The Wisdom of Oz, which brings a well-known story to a modern office setting, is a fable written for anyone who is looking for insight and guidance on how to advance their career. Stories that excite and entertain provide a great way for us to learn. They help us understand and reflect on our situation, challenges and priorities.

Perhaps that's the greatest lesson from *The Wisdom of Oz*: find learning and opportunity in unexpected places, view life and career as two parts of the same whole, and remember, above all, it's about you and the journey as much as the destination.

Jeremy Kourdi
Business Coach and Managing Director
Kourdi Ltd.

1

Dorothy

"Put your life and your future in the best
hands there are – your own"

Frank Baum

People tend to remember me because of my hair. It isn't
something I'm particularly pleased about, but I have to
accept that it's my most noticeable physical feature. The
rest of the way I look is what you might call normal. My
height is average, my eyes look like everybody else's, even
my weight and physical make up are just normal. Every
day you'll see hundreds of people who're just like me. To
tell the truth, when you look in the mirror in the morning,
the person you're looking at looks pretty much like me.
That's why I like my hair, and not just because it's long or
soft, which it certainly is. I like my hair because that's why
people notice me, remember me and take notice of what
I have to say at any given moment. It gives power to my
words and helps me to get my message across. There's no
doubt about it, it's the first thing people see of me, and the
last thing they forget about me.

Everybody says that I'm a nice person, hard working and
quite excellent at my work. I'm very focussed, and if it should
happen that I lose motivation, I can always think of a reason
to get right back into the job and concentrate on achieving my
goals. But they also say I'm too easy going, and sometimes I
let people get me down. Until today, that is.

My name is Dorothy. I've been living in New York for nearly a year, and today I'm going to take a decision that is certain to change my whole life and the lives of everyone around me. Today I'm going back to Kansas.

Of course, if you hadn't already guessed it, my hair is red.

2

The Tornado

"Opportunities are like sunrises.
If you wait too long, you miss them"

William George Ward

I can still remember how it all began. I'd only been back in Kansas a few months, in the town where I'd lived since I was very young. I loved the hot summers, liked to have an ice cream while I waited in Wyandotte Park for my father, who would have just finished working at the General Motors plant. I liked to watch the ducks splashing about on the lake, and then at five in the afternoon scores of men wearing their blue factory overalls would pour into the park with kisses and hugs for their wives and children. Dad loved to fool around with me, counting my freckles, and we would always end up laughing. He always used to tell me that since I spent my days jumping and running, my freckles would get bounced off and the number would change from one day to the next. We'd talk for ages about how I felt and what I'd done in school that day. But he never talked about his working day in the factory, even when I grew up and was mature enough to have understood what he could have told me. When I realised how hard the work was, I admired him all the more because he was always so happy with me.

Every afternoon when we strolled home we would find my mother waiting with a smile on her lips. And every day she gave my father a big hug and a passionate kiss on the lips.

I now understand that, even though when I was just a child this would make me blush, it was important for them to show the regard they had for each other, and how much it matters that we show our affection for people whom we love every chance we get. Just as they do.

My mother was a history teacher at Piper High School. She loved showing off about the marks I got and how imaginative my stories were in the literature class. Although she never stopped believing that my head was always too full of dreams, she was really proud when I decided to study advertising at Kansas University. You could tell how delighted she was when she was combing her lovely auburn hair that first morning of class, watching me with new eyes and telling me how I should behave to make an excellent first impression.

Slowly my school years passed by, marked by the usual questions and mysteries that fill the head of a young girl. My parents, always concerned for my education, did their best to answer my questions as quickly as possible with simple and understandable arguments. I loved to think that they knew everything, and to test them I used to find harder and harder questions to answer.

So it happened that I ended up at university, almost without noticing. My time as a student was almost the same as anybody else's. A lot of studying, a lot of time spent in the parks that surrounded the campus and long afternoons of exchanging confidences and laughing with my classmates. I recall that when it came to exam time I always had a tiny wound on my lower lip, because, as everyone who knows me is aware, I tend to bite it when I'm feeling nervous. If my family or friends saw that little wound they would know that I was having a hard time, and that I had something on my mind that was out of the ordinary. But I always wanted to be there for them if any of them needed me.

Thanks to good grades and a really good end-of-course project, when I finished my degree I was lucky enough to be taken on by a big local company, Uncle Henry's Farm. It was strange for a marketing firm to have a name like that, but it did the trick;

none of the customers who used its services ever forgot the name. Everybody knew that Henry Baum was a perfect boss, and that's how he got to be called Uncle Henry. The first thing I remember about him was how he looked at you. He had these blue-grey eyes that, when they settled on you, made you feel as though you were resting on a comfortable cloud. The fact that he was extremely thin, and his long greying hair, gave you the feeling that he could be a very delicate individual, but that illusion vanished as soon as he spoke. His voice was deep and serious, and made you feel that he was full of understanding and wisdom. He liked to stare out of his window, and watch people walking up and down the broad space of Washington Avenue. He always used to say, "If you watch them carefully, you can work out exactly what it is they want, and don't you forget it, Freckles". Of course, he had to travel a lot, and he was away from the office very often, but when he was around, I really learned fast. He lived his profession as though it were actually a part of his being. He once confessed to me that he intended never to retire, because "what am I going to do with my time? Retirement is for old people". It made me smile, because the first time he said it he was already over sixty-five.

From my very first day in the job he took me under his wing, and he always called me by his pet name for me, Freckles. Henry Baum led his team with affection and understanding. He always made sure you had the time you needed to understand your duties, and when he got you to do anything, you felt that he was right there, watching you and supporting you in your work. I loved the way he delegated what had to be done. Before he did it, you could see him at his desk preparing the situation, deciding whether it was right or not to pass that job down, and who would be the best person to do it. Then he used to come up really casually, and explain clearly and accurately what you needed to know: what the job was, when it should be ready, and what were the guidelines you should work within. Then he'd go over it a few more times to make sure you'd clearly understood and that you were quite sure about it. Even when he was giving you a few suggestions about how you could do the job more efficiently, he would still stay by to listen, and if you weren't convinced, he'd

explain the reasoning. It was a fact that, even though the company was small, it was very busy, and meant that Henry was very often obliged to delegate important work, but work that others could take charge of. He never stopped working, and if he did delegate something, it was because it was physically impossible for him to handle everything. One thing used to surprise me, which was that he always managed to find a minute to help and supervise if the job was going well. As he used to put it, "it's irritating to find a worm in an apple, but it's even more irritating to find half a worm".

The ten years that I worked for Uncle Henry's Farm in Kansas were ten really happy years. Even though I had my degree, I experienced almost all the departments in the business, starting as a work-experience student, then passing through the commercial and production departments until I finally got the job I wanted so much: creative manager. That was what Henry wanted.

In that job I was learning more and more every day, and thanks to the famous, albeit rare, comments from Uncle Henry, I became an advertising professional. One of his quotes that I liked best was "the best works of art in the world can never be seen if the doorman doesn't put the lights on". On the first day I thought I'd understood that what he was talking about was the importance of team work. Later on I thought he was referring to the need to understand the value of all the functions and participants in a project, since without their collaboration you could never see the job from the point of view of its full potential. Whatever he really meant, I always understood that if you don't work you can never achieve what you want to, and that it's crucial to factor in even the most obvious details.

One morning Uncle Henry called me into his office, gave me a seat and than sat down at my side, not in his usual place behind the desk. He looked at me affectionately and said:

"Good morning, Freckles. How did you sleep?"

"Like a log. The job we're working on at the moment means I'm pretty tired when I get home."

"I can imagine!" he chuckled. "What I'm sure about it that your work has been excellent. Anyway, that's what I wanted to talk to you about."

"Has there been some problem?" I was a bit worried.

"No, nothing on that score. Anyway, you know that I'm really happy with your work. But as Ralph Nader said, the job of a good leader is to create more leaders, not more followers. A couple of hours ago I got a call from Oz Company wanting to know about your availability". He calmly looked into my eyes.

"My availability? I don't get you".

"Sure Freckles, let me explain. You know that Oz Company is an advertising and marketing multinational based in New York. The President, Frank Wizard, is an old pupil of mine, and when I found out that they were looking for someone new to take over the position of creative manager, I had no hesitation in giving him a ring and mentioning you".

"But, Henry, I'm really happy right here", I said, slightly piqued.

"I know that, but this is a unique opportunity. I'm not in a position to give you the status you deserve. You've worked really hard, and your team can't speak too highly of you. When I look at you, I see enormous potential, and I don't want you to be hidden down here. You'll never be able to show your real brilliance with us. In my opinion Oz Company is a new adventure, and if you keep on working with them as you have done here, you can reach heights you could never have dreamed of. And think how proud of you I'll be".

"I'm really touched, Henry, but you can understand my hesitation. Why me? What will I do there? Where will I live? What's going to happen at the Farm?"

"Dorothy. You arrived here in my company ten years ago with the training that you get from university, good on theory but a little out of touch with reality. But you grew and you've shown on many occasions what you can really do. Do you remember in the car campaign when we suggested we could marry precision and technology with the flexibility and adaptability of oriental wisdom? Or when you suggested the advert 'For all' for the drinks campaign? The question isn't 'why you?'. It should be, 'how have we managed to take advantage of you for so long?' As regards working conditions and any other doubts you may have, I'm sure I can solve all that. But first, let me tell you a story…"

Henry Baum loved stories and anecdotes. Most of them were made up by him on the spot, but they all left you with the impression he intended. They illuminated his explanations, and according to him, they kept his mind young.

That morning, he looked me in the eyes, and began:

"I would have been barely fourteen years of age when a circus came to our town, the great Maslow circus. A few days before, all the streets had been plastered with posters advertising the incredible spectacle of the tigon, an animal that was half lion, half tiger. There was the giantess and the amazing human cannon ball, too. It was a unique show. You would never be able to see all these amazing prodigies of nature together anywhere else.

All the children in the town were extremely excited about the arrival of the Maslow circus and we missed no opportunities to persuade our parents to take us to see it. My parents, who didn't have much money, promised to take me to see it along with my three elder brothers.

The day that the big top went up I ran home from school to tell my parents, but when I got home I found my father with his head in his hands on the living room table with a very sad look on his face. He said that he hadn't been able to get together enough money, and that he only had enough for three tickets. I did some mental arithmetic and worked out that including my mother and father, we were going to need six tickets.

Without hesitation I grabbed my bike and pedalled off to the town centre. I remembered that in the antique shop window there had been a notice stating that they needed an apprentice. Naturally, I would have like to keep playing with my friends in the street and down by the river bank in the afternoons, but at least, if I got this job I would be able to get together the money we were short of.

I talked with the antique dealer, and not only did he give me the job, but he promised to advance me the first three weeks wages so that I could go to the circus with my family.

I was so thankful and happy because I'd fixed it so that the whole family could go to the circus. Although my father was a little disappointed because he hadn't been able to keep his word, nevertheless he looked at my delighted face and said "You'll always get what you want whenever you remember the tigon."

It turned out that the show was amazing, Freckles. I could barely believe my eyes.

That was why, when the show ended, I asked my Dad if we could go over to the caravans and meet the artists, and see these amazing things close up.

But that was a bad mistake. The human cannon ball turned out to be two twins wearing identical clothes, so that one got into the cannon, then there was a bang, and the other appeared at the other side of the big top. The giantess was nothing more than a dress made out of bread paste with a plump lady inside, and the tigon was just a huge lion on which someone had painted some stripes with boot polish. When my father realised this, he felt he had to cheer me up, but when he saw my face he asked me:

"Hey, son, why the smile?"

"The whole thing has been incredible," I replied, delighted.

"Explain," said my father, who didn't understand.

"It really would have been amazing if there had been a tigon, a giantess and a human cannon ball, but what's more incredible is that these are just ordinary people who've managed to persuade the world that they're real prodigies of nature. That's something that none of the kids know".

For a long time this was my second big secret, and it taught me that it's the work of a genius to persuade people to believe what we want them to believe. I think that this is the reason why, many years later, I decided to go into advertising.

During the following weeks I was completely happy working for the antique dealer, and I recall that, because of the stories that attached themselves to the objects, sales went through the roof. You didn't sell a hat, you sold the hat that a young man from the outskirts of Liverpool had been wearing the day that he first kissed his girlfriend, a young lady from Bristol who was devoted to the music of the cello. Because of the emotion of the moment they couldn't do anything about that gust of wind that carried the hat away to our own times, after floating on the breeze for years, kept aloft by the spirit of that first kiss.

In the end the antique dealer offered me a permanent job in the shop, and when I became a student I kept on working for him and helping him to become the top antique business in the city".

"Now you're face to face with this circus, Freckles. Mine taught me how to become what I am today, a successful businessman. What's yours going to teach you?"

It was a known fact that Henry's stories almost always succeeded in inspiring you and giving you a fresh injection of energy.

"What I do know now is that having heard your story I don't need to think it over. And since I know you're behind me, I'll do it – I'll go to Oz Company. Many thanks for having got me this chance," I told him, feeling really excited.

"Forget it, I'm certain I'll feel really proud that I did," he replied with a huge smile.

"Just one thing, Henry," I said as he led me to the door, "You said that the story of the circus was the second big secret of your life. May I ask what was the first?"

I knew perfectly well that Henry added these elements into his stories to create expectation, so I gave him the pleasure of answering me:

"Dorothy, when you achieve a great deed, I shall be only too pleased to tell you the story of the invisible magician."

I smiled and noticed that his eyes had begun to look misty as he said goodbye to me. As I left the office, I understood. Henry Baum had made a great sacrifice to help me achieve my success and that I now had to be strong and become the special person he said I was. I was not going to let him down, but more important, I was not going to let myself down.

Ladies and Gentlemen of Oz Company, you've just hired a woman who knows what she wants and what's more important, she's going to get it.

3

The Welcoming Committee

*"I'm a great believer in luck and I've discovered
that the harder the job, the luckier I get"*

Stephen Leacock

The next two weeks flew by. Long telephone conversations with the personnel staff at Oz Company; closing down the projects I was working on with Uncle Henry; explanations to family and friends; more phone calls... I now realised how much this change was going to mean for all those close to me, but I'd decided to take the step, and I held my ground.

The first thing I realised when the taxi I'd taken from La Guardia airport was moving through Manhattan was that this was nothing like Kansas.

There were huge avenues the like of which I'd never seen before, buildings which disappeared into the clouds, and people in their hundreds and thousands. If they weren't hanging onto their briefcases, they were talking on their cell phones. Some even had the phone in one hand and the briefcase in the other. And cars, cars, cars. There was a tide of yellow taxis, almost like a huge yellow snake crawling through the city. Then the Cuban taxi driver stopped the car and snapped:

"Thirty-five dollars."

"What?" I said, coming back to earth.

"Oz Company, thirty-five dollars," he repeated.

"I'm sorry, I don't understand."

The speed with which he spoke was so fast that I couldn't catch what he meant.

"First time in the city, right?" he smiled.

"Yes… yes. Is it so obvious?" I said, slightly put out.

"Okay, listen, I'll give you a word of advice that you'll never forget. In the city everything can have another meaning. Keep your eyes open, and never trust first impressions. Always try to find out if something else is going on," he said, trying to sound mysterious.

"Thanks, I'll bear that in mind," I replied.

"That'll be thirty-five dollars, please."

"For the advice?" I said, amazed.

"No, honey, for the ride!"

I felt like a complete idiot and my cheeks were burning. I paid the bill, thanked him and got out of the cab.

And there I was, right in front of the Oz Company offices, one of the biggest advertising and marketing multinationals in the world. The building said it very clearly: fifty-eight floors of emerald glass crowned by the letters OZ. The story goes that Frank Wizard, the owner, managed to build himself this empire thanks to the new technologies market. When he arrived in New York from Kansas he presented himself to the Singular Globe Company and offered them this deal: he would design a campaign for them and would only charge for each new client that the company won.

Naturally, the company, specialising in services for the single, thought that it was signing the business deal of the century: a marketing campaign which, if it failed, would lose them nothing. But Frank had it all worked out. On his computer he designed a campaign focusing on the sole idea of the pleasure of getting something better and the need to register to find out what it was. He started to distribute it through his lists of email addresses, internet forums and blogs. And in just a few days he had managed to get the product to take off as an advert to hundreds of thousands of users. In a month millions of notices were up and running and new customer registrations had reached two hundred thousand.

In the wake of this operation there were many who copied the format, but Frank kept on making innovations using the possibilities which technology made available to him. The search for new products, the desire to always keep on creating new markets meant that in the end he had created an empire which today is practically invulnerable. Many people claim that Frank Wizard actually doesn't exist. Others think he can get you to buy everything you never needed, as though by magic. The only thing I know is that Henry had been his teacher long before all this happened, and that right now I'm walking through the doors of his imposing building, crossing the huge entrance hall under the letters of his famous slogan "Greatness lies in simple ideas". If Frank could achieve all this, coming from Kansas, surely that means that there ought to be plenty of chances for me to do something big in New York, doesn't it?

I fantasised for a few seconds as I crossed the hall, imagining that this could all be mine. The interior of the building was amazing. The white walls which were showing dozens of screens with the weather, the news and Oz Company's latest advertisements woke me from my reverie and I began to try to imagine who all the people crossing the hall were. A giant screen was showing corporate videos and informing us that in the next few days the arrangements for the annual company trip would be finalised. This year they were going to Honolulu. My face must have been radiating bliss when a friendly woman came up to me. She was dark in complexion, with high cheekbones and a smile that split her face in two. Her suit jacket was white and she was wearing a golden name badge.

"Excuse me, can I help you?"

"Yes, of course, I'm sorry. I'm Dorothy Grimm. I've come to start my new job."

"Miss Grimm, how nice to meet you!" she said cheerfully.

"Good heavens! Do you know my job?" I asked her with curiosity.

"Your job? Well, actually, no, but in view of the fact that your arrival has led to the departure of –"

"Miss Toto!" interrupted a short-tempered security officer wearing a tight black suit who was carrying a pile of documents from one side of the hall to the other.

"Yes, Mr. Monk, I'll be right there to give you a hand. This is – look, Dorothy, take the elevator up to the twelfth floor. When you come out of the elevator look out for the creative department. When you get there your colleagues will take you to your office. I will tell Miss Heidi North that you have arrived, and she'll come over to see you in a couple of minutes. Good luck, and don't hesitate to call me if you need me!" she said, shaking my hand and leaving to help the unpleasant Mr. Monk.

I wondered what she had meant. Who or what had left because of my arrival? I turned towards the elevators and noticed that all were made of glass except one which was yellow and gold. As I approached a saw a middle-aged man with a comical moustache standing near, looking me up and down. He stopped me.

"Where do you think you're going?" he asked grumpily.

"I'm taking the elevator, if it's all the same to you," I dryly replied.

"This is the yellow elevator, no-one takes the yellow elevator."

"Why?" I asked more calmly, wanting to know.

"The yellow elevator goes straight to the area occupied by Mr. Frank Wizard, the owner of the business," he answered with an air of reverence.

"Oh, I see. I'm sorry, I didn't know. I have to go up to floor twelve, to the creative department. I'm the new manager," I smiled.

"That's okay, Miss, all the glass lifts will do, but take this," he said as he pointed to one of them, "this will take you closer to your office."

"Thanks very much," I replied as I walked into the elevator.

As I was watching the people moving about in the entrance hall I found myself remembering Alejandro Casona's statement that "there is nothing you can't say with a smile". Up went the elevator and I was then able to see just how big the building was. The huge white columns and the green glass of the windows communicated a pleasant feeling of purity and peace. The elevators rose and fell at high speed. I hardly had time to take notice of the fact that I was moving before – "Floor twelve" said an automatic voice. "Thanks," I replied, well aware that it was a machine.

Just in front of me a notice showed that that the creative department was to the left. I moved in that direction and when I opened the smoked glass doors I experienced the unquestionable power you have working in a business such as this. I was standing in a large circular room which was surrounded by some twenty white tables. They were large, equipped with all the latest IT equipment and each had a comfortable chair. I was surprised to see that everything was tidy, except for the fact that some of the work stations were scattered with piled of films and cartoons which added a pleasantly colourful note. In the centre of the room was a table containing videogames and some chairs around them with games of skill. At the side was a basketball basket with the name Oz painted on the board.

"Miss Grimm, welcome!" said a young man at the side of the room.

"Thanks," I replied.

There were around a dozen people in the room, all about my age. They certainly looked happy. One of the girls immediately said:

"We're really pleased you've got here."

"And we're delighted to know that you're our new boss, Miss Grimm," said another young woman.

"Well, you've taken me by surprise and thanks so much for the welcome, but please, call me Dorothy," I said, somewhat confused.

"Hey, how did you expect us to welcome you? You've managed to do something amazing," added a fourth.

"Me? But I've only just got here," I said, amazed, with no idea what they were talking about.

"They're saying it's your arrival at Oz Company that was the cause of departure of Mrs. East," said a really attractive woman who had just come in behind me. "Good morning, I'm Heidi North. They just told me you had arrived."

Heidi North was a blond and very beautiful woman. She wore an excellent white pinstripe suit and almost flat shoes. Even so, she was still very tall and she seemed to exude a sense of serenity.

"Miss North, I'm delighted to meet you at last! I have to tell you that the explanations you gave me over the phone were crucial for the decision I took," I added gratefully.

"The fact is that we all have great hopes for you, Dorothy. We know what you can do, and we're at the ready for you to organise your team," she said in a soft, comforting voice.

"Just getting rid of Mrs. East would be good enough," said the young man who had welcomed me, while everyone smiled and nodded.

"The fact is that she was a witch, she kept the department on the job much longer than is allowed and the pressure resulted in people being away from their stations for health reasons. She saw her colleagues as pawns in a chess game. Her fanaticism for getting up the ladder meant that she told lies on more than one occasion. She was always questioning the merits of the team and when a production problem appeared she just washed her hands of it," commented the youngest member of the group.

"Well, at least, with that attitude, she must have at least achieved her goal, right?" I asked Heidi North.

"My dear Dorothy, take a look at this computer. It is without a doubt one of the most powerful in the world. Would you be able to do good work if we took the table away from underneath it? The characteristics of the computer wouldn't have changed, but you certainly wouldn't be able to get the same out of it because of how uncomfortable you'd be, right? On top of that her credibility expired just at the moment when Mr. Wizard told me about how talented a young lady from Kansas was," she said smiling and starting to move away. "And now, please, let's stop talking about Mrs. East and get you settled into her office."

At the end of the room a wonderful office with glass walls was waiting for me. The chair seemed extraordinarily comfortable, the wide screen was huge and a library with the most cutting-edge advertising archives was furnished with an emerald green couch. Even so, I stopped for a second and asked:

"Miss North, are these tables unoccupied?" I pointed to the vacant workstations.

"That's where some of the members of your department work. The empty ones are like that because the staff members are under medical supervision or they haven't been taken over since the last time Mrs. East took to sacking people. Why?" she asked, puzzled.

"It's like this, Miss North. I want to be fully versed as regards the job, but from what I've been told it seems that this office was occupied for quite some time by someone who liked to keep her distance. I'm starting to work here like just another employee and for the moment I'm content to get by with the same tools as the rest of my colleagues. We'll use this wonderful office for meetings, and we can use her equipment whenever we need it."

"If that's what you want, so be it. And please, call me Heidi," she said, with a smile that radiated pleasure.

"Excuse me, I have a package here for the head of the creative department." We were interrupted by a fast-moving mailman talking almost at the same time as the department doors opened.

"What could that be?" wondered Heidi.

"It's a package from Mugatu Design for the head of the creative department," he replied.

"Mugatu Design is the company that this department ran its most recent campaign for. The marketing departments are in the habit of giving us some little token of recognition of our work once the campaign is complete," she explained.

"What a shame that Mrs. East can't enjoy her present," I said.

The note says "Thanks for a job well done. We would like this to stand as an indication that we are sure to hire you for our next campaign" read Heidi while she opened the package.

We were all quite taken aback at the way Heidi North's white suit reflected the glow of the package.

"If it's a present for the upcoming campaign for the head of the creative department, it's for you, Dorothy."

While she spoke she was taking a pair of fantastic, red, high-heeled shoes from the package. The cut was excellent and the stitching perfect. The colour was intense and for a moment it seemed as though the whole of the white room was bathed in colour. I had never seen such beautiful shoes.

"Thank you so much, but are you sure?" I asked.

"As sure as I am that you'll make it here. Enjoy them!" she said, handing them over to me.

Never in my wildest dreams could I have imagined a reception like this. Not only was the work environment wonderful, so were my colleagues, Miss Toto, Heidi North… everything was fantastic. The atmosphere in the office seems to imbue me with a desire to get started, and on top of everything they had given me a pair of amazing red shoes, the like of which I could never have afforded on my normal salary. At that moment I was completely happy – it had only taken a couple of hours for me to know that I had made the right decision. I already felt like a part of Oz Company.

"That's not fair!"

A piercing voice filled the room. My colleagues suddenly started to look very serious and moved away while a tall, very dark, woman moved towards me from the back of the room, walking in a way that made her look as though she was hardly lifting her feet from the floor. She seemed to be gliding. She was wearing a tailored suit cut to show off her excellent figure. Purple high-heeled shoes and a matching handbag completed the picture. Her dark eyes, surrounded by bluish mascara, and her sculpted lips delicately touched with mauve indicated a high level of concern for her image.

"I'm sorry, what were you saying?" asked Heidi politely, moving between us.

"I wondering, Miss North, what this red-headed kid is doing with those shoes" she spat, looking me up and down.

"Allow me to introduce Dorothy Grimm, the new creative manager of Oz Company."

"New creative manager? Impossible, I have given my approval to no such thing" she snapped with fury.

"I'm sorry, but this is a personal decision made by Mr. Wizard himself," she smiled broadly.

"Frank? I find that… highly unlikely."

"Mrs. East's position was vacant, so the company needed a new creative manager. In the light of the excellent work done by Dorothy, and since the human resources manager, another company officer, felt this was an appropriate candidate, the result is what you see," she calmly explained.

"We shall see about that… And anyway, what about those shoes?"

"What about the shoes?" asked Heidi placidly.

"Just this. It is unfair for the new arrival to keep those shoes from Mugatu. I was involved in that campaign, and it is thanks to me that it succeeded. So, since Mrs. East is unable to enjoy them, it would appear logical that another manager who took part in the campaign should have them. The financial director, in other words, an officer of the company."

"Mrs. West, I understand your reasoning, but the fact is that Mugatu Design obviously sent the shoes to the creative manager, and that happens to be Dorothy. There isn't any doubt about that. This young lady is the legitimate owner."

"Really, it doesn't matter…" I murmured.

"Stay cool, Dorothy, Mrs. West was just on the way to her department. If I understand correctly you have to balance the figures for the last quarter, and that is a lot of accounts, right?"

"Unbelievable! So this small-town hick gets the shoes! She wouldn't know how to wear them! Well, let me tell you pair a thing or two. In a short while you'll find you have to get me to pass a budget proposal to cover an increase in staff numbers, or it might just be for a new box of pens. I may find myself in a generous mood, or then again…"

"I'm sorry, Mrs West. The decision has been taken. The shoes belong to Dorothy" Heidi firmly interrupted her.

"Fine! Fine! I think you'll find you've made a big mistake. The day will come when you're begging me to take those shoes. The lean times are on the way for you and your people, so you'd better get ready to tighten your belts."

She spun round with an air of majesty. Even though I didn't want to feel it, her fury was palpable. Even as she stormed out of the door she nearly sent spinning a colleague who was just coming in.

"Really, Heidi, she could have taken the shoes... I mean, after all, I've only just got here," I said in an effort to smooth things over.

"I know, Dorothy, but you mustn't forget that people have got to take you seriously. It isn't just your work alone that people will know you by. It's a sad fact that if you let people like Mrs West and one or two others in this building walk all over you, they will never let you evolve and develop. They'll change you into a grey nonentity, a doormat. And we've hired you so that we can bask in your colours. Anyway," she added as she left the office, "everybody knows that the finance department is the eternal enemy of advertisers, don't they?"

Heidi North's words echoed in my brain. There were sure to be people here who would not only not support me, but who would in fact be out to see me fail. I had to stop thinking like a kid from Kansas fast and get a hold of the fact that this was New York, more precisely it was Oz Company, and things were very, very different.

I took another look around me, making a careful note of the equipment and offices, glanced at the huge windows and then turned back to my colleagues who were all watching me.

"Well, then," I said with a smile on my face, "maybe someone could bring me up to date with what's going on in the department?"

Time to go to work.

4

The Meeting with Boq

"Uncertainty is a daisy with petals
which never stop falling"

Mario Vargas Llosa

The next few days passed by relatively smoothly. My colleagues explained previous advertising campaigns to me, how the department worked and what each person's speciality was. They really were a nice bunch, genuinely motivated by my presence in the department, and I was ready to give them all the time they needed.

In those early weeks I learned that my team was a large group of quite young people with excellent training and focus, and a great appetite for hard work. You could say that I had everything that a boss could ask for.

One morning, Boq, the creative department viral marketing expert, took time out to explain exactly how he operated and why he was one of the most highly thought-of members of the section. I paid careful attention to what he was saying, and a logical question suddenly came into my head which, judging by his reaction, was also somewhat unexpected.

"So does Frank Wizard oversee our end job?"

"Mr. Wizard?" he said in surprise.

Boq had been working with the company since he started in the business and he was the member of my team who knew Oz Company best.

"Well, you know, it's just that, since he is the owner of the company I wondered if he had any power of veto over the campaigns," I said, trying to make my question a little clearer.

"Dorothy, Frank Wizard hasn't supervised a job in over three years. Since he set up the board of directors, he's disappeared. You can send him an email, and you'll get an answer, but the story is that it's just from a secretary whose job is to deal with them."

"But how is that possible? Only the other day, Heidi North told me that it had been he himself who had recommended me for the position."

"It's like this, Dorothy, all the members of the board of directors talk about him as though he really is there and they see him every day. The entire company assumes he's there working away, but the fact is that no-one ever sees him enter or leave the building. He's never seen in the cafeteria, and any time there's a trip or company dinner you can be sure that Frank Wizard will have a perfectly credible excuse or something unavoidable will have come up at the last minute."

"But is there any solid evidence about what he's doing, or is there just gossip?"

"What can we say? Common sense knows that this company was built up on a basis of creativity, innovation and a painstakingly detailed knowledge of the brands in question."

"Not forgetting the undeniable commercial success of the campaigns," I put in.

"Sure, we have to acknowledge the fact that the brands we cover have always achieved sales increases greater than expected. Even so, in the last few months some odd things have been happening at Oz Company. Budgets are becoming increasingly important, and it seems now as though we get a new policy every day focussing on the development of our own brand to the detriment of our concern for the clients. Probably the biggest news is that in the upcoming months we're going to see a big move to expand into other states."

"Is that unusual?" I asked, not quite seeing where he was going.

"Frank Wizard would never have approved of this kind of strategy. He always believed in dealing fairly with the competition, in offering our services, sure, making money out of that, but he never wanted to dominate the market. He always used to say 'Oz Company will be the odd man out in the market, the joker in the pack, an albino tiger in a zoo full of colourful animals. We shall be original, different, unique and small. That is what will make us great'. Frank wanted us to be known by the originality and profitability of our campaigns, not by the size of the company."

"But Oz Company is already a multinational" I put in.

"His ideas are universal and that's why he has multinational clients. But this intention to erupt into a new expansion strategy is very unlike his ideas. It doesn't match the way Frank thinks. He believed in ideas, not empire."

"Just hang on a second!" I said, seeing a possible solution. "My old boss, Henry Baum, was Frank's teacher and he called him to say that I was available. Just give me a minute, let's see if he can explain it."

While Boq was gazing at me open-mouthed because of my decision, I took my cell phone out of my bag and called Uncle Henry. In a moment or two a voice which seemed very nearby and reassuring came on the line.

"Hey, Freckles! How's the big city treating you?"

"I can't complain! The fact is that it's like a dream," I answered, moved at hearing his voice.

"I'm delighted to hear it. I always knew that you were destined for this kind of work."

"Thanks, Henry, but I'm really missing you," I said rather sadly.

"Get away! That lasts just until you're into the routine of the job and have got to know all the people. By the way, have you met the board yet?"

"That's what I wanted to talk to you about. When you were explaining the details of the job to me, you said that you'd talked with Frank, right?"

"To tell you the truth, when I'd called him a few times and never managed to get through direct, we closed the deal by email. I guess that's pretty normal in a business the size of his. Why do you ask?"

"Nothing, really, it's nothing. I just wanted to know if you'd been in contact with him. It's always good to keep in touch, right?"

I really didn't want to bother him. Maybe it was all nothing at all, and anyway I knew that Henry had enough problems in his daily work without upsetting him with mysteries. We chatted for a few more minutes about how our lives were going on, and then I thought it was time to ring off.

"OK, Henry, I have to get back to work. Say hi to everybody for me, and tell them that I'll be visiting as soon as I can."

"Do you think you'd be able to make it to the meeting?"

"What meeting?" I didn't know what he was talking about.

"The meeting I shall be having with the Oz Company representatives. It seems they want to establish some partnership arrangements with some of the businesses in Kansas. If it works out okay they'll be able to offer us some of their clients who have subsidiaries in this area. I assumed that the fact that I'd sent you there was beginning to bear fruit. Collaboration is the foundation of success, Freckles, and don't you forget it."

"That sounds fantastic. Who told you about the meeting?"

"Well, I got a letter with Frank's signature on it, although he did say that he wouldn't be able to make it in person. It seems he has to take a trip to Europe. He'll be represented by... just a moment, I've got it jotted down here. Ah, yes, a Mrs. West."

"Mrs. West?" My heart skipped a beat. "Uncle Henry, when does this meeting take place?"

"It's down for next week. Is there something I ought to know, Dorothy?" Henry asked, picking up on my unease.

"I'm not sure yet. Mrs. West is giving off really bad vibes. Is there any chance of postponing the meeting?"

"All of a sudden it looks as though my diary is really full. Would some time in the next, say, six weeks suit you?" He was trying to calm me down.

"Many thanks, Henry, but look, it's probably nothing. I'll keep you posted."

"Okay, Freckles. And you take care, now."

There's nothing like finding you can create trust in the hearts of others. He could do it for me, too. He hadn't hesitated for a second to accede to my request. Maybe it was because we were so close, maybe because we had never let each other down, or perhaps it was just because when we made a mistake or were feeling out on a limb, we never tried to hide anything from each other. The outcome was that I had gained a few weeks in which time I could try to find out precisely what Mrs. West was up to.

"It looks as though we have two mysteries on our hands," I said to Boq.

"Two?" he asked in some confusion.

"Yes. So it turns out that he's someone else who didn't speak directly with Frank, and contact was by email. So the first thing we need to know is whether Frank Wizard is really here and running the wonderful Oz Company."

"I guess you'll find that out soon enough."

"How come?" I was puzzled.

"Simple. You're the new creative manager, and according to the articles of association, once you've got through the six month settling-in period, you take your seat on the board. It's part of the job. Although, of course, it's possible that once you're there you may decide to abide by the board's decisions and carry on as though nothing were happening."

"That's fantastic," I said, relieved. "In just a few months I'll be on the board and we'll find out at last what's really going on. And don't worry, you'll know the truth. You'll always get the truth from me."

"I believe you. So what's the other problem?" He looked concerned.

"It turns out that Mrs. West wants to have a meeting with Uncle Henry to set up a business relationship between his company and Oz Company. But that sounds weird to me. I don't have a good feeling about it. I suspect she may have other plans. Henry Baum really loves his company, and if anything were to happen…"

"I think you're right to be worried. For over a year now Mrs. West's power in the company has been growing out of all proportion. Nobody dares question her decisions and her intentions are far from clear. If we used to have a witch in our department, well, she's got to be the witch's elder sister."

"You know what, Boq? This all reminds me of a story that Uncle Henry once told me. Can I share it with you?"

"A story? Sure, I can always learn something new." He made himself comfortable in his seat.

> "Long, long ago, the Sultan of Bail-Bag was furious," I began my tale. "Desertions from the ranks of the army were continually increasing. The news of an enemy invasion became more urgent every day, since everybody knows that Bail-Bag is an oriental island located in a very rich and prosperous position. Its wines were famous through the whole of the Mediterranean. Following many time-wasting meetings, a counsellor whom the Sultan thought very highly of because of his wise counsel asked him to perform a test.

He order a soldier to be locked up in an empty room, the four walls of which were painted white, and where the only thing which stood out was the colour of the doors. There was a door in each wall. The counsellor said to the soldier: 'Now, choose your fate'. The soldier looked carefully at the doors and then, after a few moments, he burst into tears and begged for mercy.

"The Sultan had no idea what was happening and asked the soldier what was the matter. The soldier came to attention and explained that he was unable to choose his fate because each door was more cruel than the previous one. If he chose the blue door, he would be drowned in a mountain torrent. If he chose the yellow door he would be abandoned in the desert of oblivion. If his decision were for the red door he would be burned at the stake of the guilty, and finally, if he chose the green door, he would be fed to the Sultan's wife's pet crocodiles.

"The Sultan turned to his counsellor and asked him whether he had told the solider all this. The counsellor shook his head, and said that he had merely told the soldier to choose his fate. The fact was that the blue door would get the soldier appointed as captain of a vessel which had the duty of visiting the neighbouring kingdoms, so that he would enjoy the best of hospitality from the people. The yellow door would load him with gold. The red door would result in the soldier becoming the representative of all the vineyards in the kingdom, so his fame would spread to the four corners of the world. And if he chose the green door he would always be attended by the best doctors, taking care of his health.

"The Sultan nodded at his counsellor and rewarded his labours with a fat bag of gold. The simple explanation was that the soldiers were deserting because they allowed their uncertainties to become peopled with their greatest fears. All they had to do was see their enemies for what they were, and not the ghosts which lived in their minds."

"We fill in our uncertainties with our fears…" Boq murmured as he jotted something down in a notebook.

"Precisely. What we need is information, so that we can fill in the spaces with real data, not suppositions or fears," I replied.

"But where do we find that information?" asked Boq, somewhat surprised to see me setting off.

"From the information desk, obviously," I smiled.

5

Dorothy Helps Oscar Crow

*"Help your fellow man to lift his burden, but
don't feel obliged to carry it for him"*

Pythagoras of Samos

I had no intention of worrying my team or making them suspicious, so I immediately took the elevator and went in search of Miss Toto in the building entrance area.

She wasn't actually at her information desk, so I took a look at the groups of people chatting in the reception hall and that was where I located her. She was chatting with a young man who appeared to be in some difficulty.

He was tall and thin, with large black eyes and a nose like a carrot. He was wearing khaki chinos and a green shirt, in fact he was dressed rather casually in comparison with the norm for Oz. Miss Toto was looking rather concerned and seemed to be trying the cheer the sad young man up.

"I really don't know what to do," he was explaining, "I'm completely trapped. Everything I try to get started is vetoed with the excuse that funds are insufficient, or the idea isn't profitable enough."

"You know that we're all in the same boat on that score, but Oscar, you're on the board. Won't anybody back you?"

"The rest of the board are just like me, I've no idea how it's turned out like this, but, with the exception of Heidi, everybody is just too worried sick about the survival of their team to try to come up with other possible options."

"Excuse me interrupting," I butted in gently, "I'll only be a moment."

"Well, I'll just carry on taking it easy, but I have to come up with an idea." He smiled at Miss Toto.

"Good luck, Oscar, I'm sure it will come out all right in the end," and she gave him a wink.

"Excuse me once again, but I have something rather urgent to ask you," I said, apologising.

"Don't worry, Dorothy, the fact is that in these cases all I can do is listen. But Oscar is so upset…"

"Oscar?" I asked.

"Yes, that young man I was talking to. His name is Oscar Crow. He's the company research and development manager. His responsibility is to generate new ideas, to create strategies, try out new lines of activity…"

"How interesting! But why is he so upset?" I wondered.

"Well, the fact is that sooner or later you'll find yourself experiencing the same situation, so it's best if you know how things are, but I hear you already know something about it on the matter of a pair of shoes," she said with a smile. "Well done!"

"With Mrs. West? How did you know about that?"

"Well, Dorothy, big though this company may be, it's really just like a small town. We all find out everything eventually, particularly if it's bad news about Mrs. West."

"It was really nothing, just a misunderstanding." I explained.

"Okay, it's like this. As you know, Mrs. West is head of the finance department, and because of her profitability policy, she's blocking the budgets of practically every department. If you want more capital, you have to fall in with her requirements."

"Her requirements?" I didn't understand.

"At each board meeting Mrs. West tables a list of resolutions and the ones that are always passed are approved on the vote of the members of the board whom she helped or promised to open the tap for."

"But that's blackmail!" I was angry.

"It's that and a great deal more. The real problem is that she needs the unanimous support of the management to get what she really wants, and while Heidi, Oscar and a few others are always there, she can never get it. But her powers are constantly growing. When she costs someone's budget, not only does she paralyse the department but she brings out into the open the staff members who disagree with her plans. Heidi has been forced to fire some of them."

"What's her game?" I wondered.

"To dominate Oz Company."

"But Frank Wizard would never allow that, would he?" I asked, worried.

"The investors make the decisions. Frank put all his money in this company to get it started years ago, and now it's the investors who decide. Although it's true that Mr. Wizard has the final say, he's obliged to accept any change in the membership of the board or the management of the company, if the majority vote is in favour."

"Talking about Mr. Wizard, has he really disappeared?"

"Who told you that?" She smiled nervously. "Frank never spent a great deal of time here, but that nothing like saying he's disappeared. He's still running the company, from wherever he happens to be, or at least, some of us hope he is."

"I'm sure that's so, Oz is his creation. Could you abandon something like this?" I said, trying to cheer her up.

"Wow, it certainly wouldn't be easy!" she smiled. "Oh, by the way Dorothy, I have a letter for you, I think it's about a new job from one of our top clients. I'll just get it for you, it's on my desk."

I took the envelope, took my leave of Miss Toto and headed for my office. I tried to forget the negative thoughts that remained in my mind. When I felt at my ease I sat down and opened the envelope which bore the famous Macrosoft butterfly logo.

Miss Grimm,

My name is Markus Mark, marketing manager with Macrosoft. First let me congratulate you on taking up your new position. I'm sure that you will be as valuable to Oz Company as we have been led to believe. Your earlier work speaks very well of you and we're proud to be able to rely on your ideas for our new campaign.

As you are no doubt aware, our company is a world leader in IT operating systems. For years we have managed to keep well ahead of our competitors, and have managed to ensure that the world of the computer is now within the reach of everybody, regardless of age, training or social status, since, thanks to the computers which include our systems, everything is much simpler.

Our values have always been effectiveness, simplicity and resource power. We hope that you will be able to continue seeing us as one more aspect of your natural environment.

In recent times our most serious competitor has been gaining ground on us because of its cutting edge design and professional credibility.

It is for this reason that, due to the upcoming launch of the upgraded version of our famous operating system, regarding which we are entrusting the campaign to you, we want to win back the hearts of the users. We need to generate within them the comfortable feeling of being adequately supported by our teams while not forgetting our well-known image and our accessibility.

*On other matters, we have always paid a great deal of
attention to the environment, and in view of the problems
of climate change, with which we are seriously concerned,
we would like this campaign to explain this concern by
including the message that if we all pull together, we can
solve it.*

*I look forward to learning what ideas you have, and take
this opportunity to once again wish you all the very best.*

Yours sincerely,
Markus Mark
Marketing Manager
Macrosoft

I continued to read all the data about the company, the specifications
and requirements for the new product and I organised a meeting
with my team to tell them about the project and to get the work
started.

One single detail had not been specified: the budget.

I checked the files to find out what the budget had been for
the previous Macrosoft campaign and found that it had been
half a million dollars. I sat down to write a note to the finance
department, to tell them about the opening of the new campaign
and the deadline the client was able to allow us. The reply came
very quickly.

Dear Miss Grimm,

*We are pleased to note the opening of the new campaign,
and would like to inform you that the finance department
is at your service.*

*However, we are sorry to have to inform you that, due to
the expansion and development policy which Oz Company
is currently implementing, we are only able to offer you a
budget for the campaign of three hundred thousand dollars.*

We are obliged to generate in-house wealth and to ensure that every project generates the maximum profit possible. We know that you believe in the future of our company and that you will therefore understand the situation.

Should you require any further information or a meeting, do not hesitate to contact me.

W. West
Financial manager
Oz Company

This was incredible. How could I possibly achieve the impact and weight required by this campaign with such a minuscule budget? Without hesitation I picked up the phone and began to speak.

"Mrs. West, good afternoon."

"Good afternoon, Dorothy, you took thirty seconds longer than I expected. I'm delighted to see that you understand the situation." Her voice dripped with sarcasm.

"Please tell me simply how you expect me to run the Macrosoft campaign on the budget you have allotted me. It is not possible." I tried to keep my voice serious.

"Remember the line that Frank Wizard made famous: 'Greatness comes from simple ideas'," she said, while in my mind's eye I knew she was smiling.

"Of course, I know, but then the ideas have to be produced and communicated."

"Then think of something suitable, because if you don't your production and communication colleagues will be unable to develop the campaign and it will be the first failure in this company."

"But I can't take on that responsibility with such a tiny budget," I snapped.

"Well, there's always another option." Her voice had taken on a silken tone. "It might always be possible to raise the budget for the campaign in return for something you have and I want."

"The shoes? It is utterly childish and pathetic of you to toy with a campaign of this size for something so trivial. You want the shoes?"

It was at that moment that I realised that all my colleagues were looking at me with a mixture of surprise and pain. I understood the importance of the shoes. They had become transformed into the hope and motivation of my companions, they were the symbol of the revolution which had just broken out. Mrs. West may have cowed the whole company, but while those shoes were in my power we would all have motivation and strength to carry on.

"As far as the shoes are concerned, Mrs. West, I'm sorry, but you will have to come up with a much better idea than that to get your hands on them," I replied with confidence.

"You have made a mistake, child. You will regret that decision," she said, promptly hanging up.

"Well done! You really are the boss!" commented some of my colleagues, and I got a round of applause.

Blushing to my boots, I got up and walked towards them.

"It would appear that Frank Wizard always said that greatness lay in simple ideas. Very well, this is our chance to prove him right. Mrs. West has decided to transform Oz Company into her own private playground. She's devoting all her energy to making sure that the rest of the teams fail, so that she will appear as the best option. Now we have a new opportunity. Macrosoft have shown their faith in us yet again to develop a new campaign.

"We all remember earlier great ideas," I said, maintaining eye contact. "We've all enjoyed extraordinary campaigns which our colleagues created, but the most important thing is that every one of us in this department is capable of creating those great ideas. This is our chance. We shall show everybody that the creative department is still on its feet. We shall come up with a brilliant, original idea, worthy of the spirit of Mr. Wizard. We shall show Oz Company that a new era has begun and that the creative department is ready for it."

I noticed, against the background of the clapping, that some of my colleagues were beginning to infect the others with their enthusiasm. They smiled at each other, hugged and swiftly grabbed their pencils and laptops, and began to process all the information that the company had supplied us with.

I knew it would not be easy, that would have to hit on something which so far had never been done to achieve a greater emotional penetration among our potential customers.

Then I remembered Oscar Crow. This was going to be a very difficult goal to achieve, and the research and development department was looking for opportunities. I found the internal telephone list and rang his extension.

"Could I speak with Mr. Crow, please?"

"This is he, and please call me Oscar. Who am I speaking with?" replied a quiet voice.

"This is Dorothy Grimm. We met before in the entrance hall. I'm the new manager of the creative department," I said with assurance in my words.

"Ah, the famous redhead! What can I do for you?" he replied in a friendly manner.

"I need the help of your department. I have to create a new idea and unfortunately my budget is very limited."

"Mrs. West?" he put in.

"Precisely. The finance department has allotted us a very inadequate budget and I have to come up with something extraordinary, something unique. That's where you come in."

"I'd love to help you, Dorothy, but I'm afraid you have the wrong guy, or at least, the wrong time. I feel as though I haven't got enough brains left to think straight. These last few months have left me with so many in-house problems that my head is fully occupied with trying to find solutions for them and to keep my department together to be able to research new formulas. I'm sorry, but I don't think I'm the brain you're looking for."

"Listen Oscar, wouldn't this be just the chance to start to turn this situation around? If we work on the new campaign your colleagues will get excited by the new project, and if, in the end we come out on top that will energise your department, and everybody will begin to value you as you deserve. The best motivation you can find is achieving small tangible successes for your people. How long is it since you gave them a win, Oscar?"

Oscar Crow was silent for a few moments before he said at last.

"Dorothy, I have to say that I really can't miss this chance. As you very rightly say, you have to have a few successes, right? Okay, let's achieve a success of major proportions. Maybe if we can do that I'll start to believe myself that I really do have the brain for this kind of work. When can we meet?"

6

The Road to Travel

"When a mistake is made by many people
it starts to look like the truth"

Gustavo Le Bon

Only a couple of days had gone by since we received
the project, but already you could sense the willingness
and enthusiasm in the air. We had all by now read the
client's guidelines several times, and had talked amongst
ourselves and compared our ideas about them. We realised
that, however well drafted they might be, we all have a
tendency to interpret them according to our own tastes and
preferences.

My team was coming up with plenty of ideas, few of which
were doable, some of which were too expensive, and there
were even some which almost fell foul of ethical standards,
but, frankly, that's what you get when you put together
twelve brilliant young minds and give free rein to their
imagination. All we had were the following guidelines: it
had to be original, something which would touch the heart,
be environmentally friendly and have a global reach. We
also had to factor the competition in, and be aware of its
strengths. A good image, an attractive logo and a fresh
message were its main strengths.

I left my team working and made my way to my meeting
with Oscar Crow. Just as I moved towards the elevators I

noticed Boq making a gesture inviting me to join him. Maybe he had found something out.

"What is it, Boq? Have you discovered something new?"

"Yes, Dorothy. It appears that Mrs. West wants to gain the trust of the investors at all costs by producing an amazing profit. She wants to show that with her at the helm of the company they will be sure to fill their pockets, and her ego will be satisfied."

"What do you mean?"

"Oz Company is going to start taking over a number of marketing companies in various states, and that's why she wants to get a lot of money together. She needs to buy a company with a good market position in each of the states she's decided on. I've managed to get hold of a list of the cities she's selected, Philadelphia, Atlanta, Boston, Springfield, Memphis and Miami."

"But that's against the original Oz philosophy!"

"Sure, but just hang on a second. Suppose the owner of MacDonald's goes to Beijing, he would be sure to want to try out one of the restaurants in his chain in Tiananmen Square, right? The feeling of pride is what she wants to stir up in the investors, she wants them to feel like Walt Disney with his tourist complexes. She wants to dominate the market not just through the campaigns, but through the economic power and size of the company."

"Understood, Boq, thanks," I said, taken aback by the information. "By the way, is Kansas one of the cities?"

"Kansas? It wasn't on the list, but I'll keep my ear to the ground."

Hearing that put me at ease for a moment, but then I began to wonder whether that was what she really wanted from Uncle Henry.

When I reached the research and development department I was surprised by the extent of the facilities. There was a room over four hundred square metres in size with a roof six metres in height. A number of screens adorned the walls showing campaigns which had never seen the light of day. One of them was projected onto a curtain of smoke generated with liquid hydrogen, while another projected a three-dimensional image of extraordinary solidity and reality. Further into the room was a plant on which every leaf was marked in a very natural way with the logo of a multinational company. But what really surprised me was there was what appeared to be a huge telescope majestically presiding over the room.

"Wow!" I exclaimed involuntarily.

"Ah Dorothy, here you are!" said Oscar, making his way towards me.

"What's that?" I asked, pointing to the telescope.

"What it is, well… I'll make it simple. Could you imagine the moon advertising a company every night?"

"What? You could project something onto the moon?" I was amazed.

"That was the idea, but as I said the other day, between shortness of staff and shortness of my ideas, I've run into a brick wall, and that's the truth. But we have other fish to fry, right?" He led me towards his office.

We chatted for a moment or two about how his department operated, and the reasons for the high level of absenteeism. He told me that if he himself was uncertain about his abilities, how could his staff fail to feel the same? Things would go from bad to worse, since the company could see that they were costing money, and that capital could be made better use of.

"Be made better use of?" I was astonished.

"That is Mrs. West's opinion. For example, a year ago we designed and built the plant you see at the entrance. The idea was to replace all the sponsorship notices which really foul up buildings, botanical gardens, zoos and the like with plants showing the logo of the company which put up the money for building or maintenance. Its originality and practical function are obvious. But in the end we couldn't sell the project because each plant cost twice the price of the metal plaque. They told us to freeze research on the project."

"But that shouldn't be a problem. It's normal for us to launch campaigns for products which are dearer," I reassured him.

"I know, but that meant we needed a sales campaign, and that's where the budget ran out. The rest you know. The joke is that we're now stuck with about a thousand plants doomed to die in this room."

"What was the company which financed it?"

"There wasn't one, Dorothy, those plants are the outcome of the first production. That was the stock we needed which was created on our budget, awaiting future clients. The genetically modified plant only needs a vitamin discharge with the logo we want to print and nature does the rest," he explained with feeling.

"Nature does the rest?"

"I'll show you," he said, picking up one of the plants, "I insert the chip with the logo, that of Oz Company for example, I administer the vitamins, sprinkle it with a little water…"

All of a sudden, a fig tree almost two metres high and with huge leaves began to look greener and as if by magic the logo of our company appeared there. The impression was fantastic, dozens of leaves with the logo printed on them.

"As you can see, the chlorophyll becomes concentrated, imitating the image which we have given it," he explained.

"But that's amazing. Does it damage the plant?"

"It's completely harmless, although we did experience a couple of problems. The first was that we couldn't get the logo to stay on the leaf for more than a month. After that, the mark would disappear, and the plant just beautifies the garden or house where it's been planted. Nothing more."

"And the second?"

"The second is this," he said, pointing out an enormous flower which had just appeared at the very top of the plant. "Several tend to come out on each plant."

It was at that moment that my brain started to come up with ideas. If we could use these plants we could create an effect which, at least to my way of thinking, would look amazing.

"You know something, Oscar? You've just solved a big problem for me," I told him excitedly. "Since you've told me that the plants are doomed, maybe I could use them in this campaign."

"Well, my team would certainly be delighted if one of our ideas were to see the light of day after such a long time. But what is the idea I've given you? I can't remember mentioning any idea," he apologised.

"You haven't had any ideas? You've made some progress here worthy of the most innovative companies. The kind of person who gets really motivated, and believes in what he does. You're a boss who's concerned about his team and you think constantly about how you can improve things. Your colleagues ought to feel proud to be working with a guy like you."

"So why are they leaving?"

"The other day we were chatting about the scoring wins in general, and I now discover that they don't feel recognised or important to the firm because the successes they achieve are then left unused. There's something else. I think your negativity is affecting them. As you told me, if you don't believe in your skills, then you don't have the necessary authority to act. You have to stop thinking that you're worthless. Look around you and try to find tangible proof of what you're saying. Would someone who never had an idea have come up with all this? Could someone who's worthless run a team capable of creating these amazing things? Get real, Oscar, if you really believe that after all you have no brains, then no-one has one."

"Thank you, Dorothy, that's the first time anyone has ever said anything like that to me," he said, rather moved. "They never talk to your about strengths and weaknesses, and you know what? I'm starting right away."

"You're welcome, Oscar. Now I have to get back to my department and tell them all about the idea that I'm hatching… and thanks. The research and development department has done its work, and what a work it is. I'll call you soon and let you know the details."

When I got back to my office everybody had assembled ready for the meeting. I told them that we had at our disposal, thanks to the research and development section, one thousand plants at zero cost. Their faces revealed no trace of emotion until I started to tell them the plants' fantastic properties. When I had finished they were delighted with our free gift.

It took only a few seconds for the ideas to start flowing.

"Magic plants!"

"If we count every leaf that makes tens of thousands of advertising supports, completely free!" put in one of the younger members of the team.

"And the effect will be fantastic!" said Boq.

"Just one moment!" interrupted another team member. "I have an idea!"

Over a period of several minutes I laid out my concept and you could see how the rest of my colleagues became fired. Some even made their own contributions to the original idea so that it would have a greater impact. When everybody clearly understood the idea, I asked:

"Do we have an idea, then?"

"No," replied Boq. "We have a campaign."

"The let's make it a great one!" I concluded.

It was marvellous to see how everyone went to work with a smile on their lips. Adaptation of the logo, views of the city parks, slogans… We all had the same vision, all with the same motivation: to create a great advertising campaign for our client. Something we could be proud of.

In the meantime I picked up the phone and called Oscar:

"It's Dorothy. How long do you need to put our logo into all the plants?"

"Well, I'll need all my team together as soon as they're planted in the final location, and then one working day."

"Hey! I don't think I can spare that kind of time. Can I collaborate using my department to help you? How much would that cut the time down by?"

"Sure, no problem, my team can take charge of the chips and yours can deal with the application of the vitamins. That will cut down the procedure. Anyway, who could really help us is the production department. Timothy Mann has been running that department for years."

"So what do you think? Can we persuade him to give us a hand?"

"Well, the fact is that that's what the production department is for, but Timothy is a very cold and calculating person. Emotions are of no interest to him. So if we want to sell the project to him, you have to emphasis other factors."

"Don't worry, I can take care of that. Could you come with me to see him tomorrow morning?" I asked as pleasantly as I could.

"With the greatest of pleasure."

That evening as I walked down Fifth Avenue towards my apartment I felt uneasy. I didn't feel like stopping for an aperitif in Blue Note, which had become my custom, or sitting opposite the university watching people making their way to the jazz clubs. That night I went straight home. I knew that something important was brewing and that I needed to rest. My lower lip was feeling the effects.

The Norrington Building was one of the first neoclassical buildings to go up in Greenwich Village. I had taken an apartment there which was very convenient for getting to the city, and I had fixed it up to suit me. Hints of chocolate and orange in the sheets and curtains, some beige throw cushions and aromatic candles could make me feel as though I was right back in Kansas.

I was just about to go to bed when suddenly I felt an irrepressible desire to see them. I opened the cupboard, took out the Mugatu Design box and carefully removed the lid. They beauty and symbolism made me take them out of the box, just to look at them for a minute. I placed them in front of the bed – it was as though they gave me strength.

I got into bed, pulled up the covers and closed my eyes while saying to myself:

"Everything is starting to take shape. Things are beginning to happen".

7

Rescuing Tim Mann

*"All men have hearts, although they
may not follow its dictates"*

Ernest Hemingway

That morning was colder than usual. It seemed as though the spring had not yet arrived. Even so, I was ready for anything, knowing that this morning would affect the way all future events would happen.

As I walked in through the Oz doors, my companion Oscar Crow was waiting for me with a huge smile on his face.

"Good morning, Dorothy, I have an idea that could be fantastic."

"Hi Oscar, can you tell me on the way up to Timothy Mann's office?" I grinned at him.

It took barely forty seconds to reach floor twenty, not enough to set out a complete overall idea, but plenty to sketch out a fair idea of it. We would use all the plants marked with the Macrosoft logo. Our final assessment was that around a thousand plants would do. A few dozen would remain in the company, for future experimentation.

I was surprised to find that the production department was dominated by aluminium tables and metal sculptures. We walked to the end of the passage and made our way into

Timothy's office. In keeping with the decorative style of his department, the office was a large metal-plated room, with a big aluminium table and a window from which you could see the huge skyscrapers which surrounded the area. Timothy Mann was sitting down contemplating that view. He was a tall, tubby man, with greying, almost silver hair. His grey suit perfectly matched the bluish tones in his tie.

"Yesterday when you called me I couldn't quite understand what you were trying to explain to me, Oscar. I'm a bit rusty," he said, while slowly raising a hand to greet us.

"Good morning, Timothy." Oscar greeted him warmly. "Let me introduce Dorothy, the new manager of the creative department."

"Good morning. Excuse my asking if it's out of turn, but what do you mean by feeling rusty?" I enquired politely.

Suddenly a small tic passed across his face. It was as though he hadn't been expecting that question, or rather had been expecting it for a long time.

"Just that. The production department is the most highly automated in the company. We aren't responsible for creating illusions, nor do we communicate by emotive means. We restrict ourselves to bringing a few people's dreams to life and ensuring that the product is operational so that others can sell it. That what our department is like. I have always known that, and have depended on it, but recent organisational changes have transformed this department, and me, into a simple bureaucratic automaton. But don't let's talk about that now, tell me what brings you here."

"It's like this, Mr. Mann," I started to explain to him, "when I arrived at the business a few weeks ago you could say that my entrance did not have a positive effect on Mrs. West..."

"Mrs. West? This is becoming interesting!" he said, turning his incredibly blue eyes on us.

"As I was saying, this didn't give rise to any specific problems at first. But now one of the company's biggest clients has just entrusted us with their new advertising campaign. They want it to communicate the foundations of their efficiency and well-known success, but they want to add a more human view of the product, with more values, particularly human and environmental values. The problem appeared when we realised what the budget was going to be, almost half what we had been provided with before."

"I know her tactics. Has she asked you for anything in exchange?" he asked, his tone becoming more familiar, while he revolved slowly towards his desk.

"If you don't mind, I'd like to keep off the subject of Mrs. West, and concentrate on the project."

"You're tough. I like that."

Timothy Mann's face bore a faint smile as he asked us to sit down. He picked up a notebook and began to note down everything we told him.

We explained the project to him, the idea of using the plants from the research and development department and the fact that we needed his help in the production of the campaign. At that moment his eyes seemed to be lost again on the horizon.

"No problem, my department is at your service. If Oscar and his team begin with the first stage of the development of the plants, my staff will be ready to execute the campaign in a couple of hours."

Many thanks, Timothy, but is everything all right?" I asked.

"No, no, everything's fine, don't worry. It's just that, as you see, the work we have to do is purely mechanical. I am, of course, an expert at that, but I don't know…"

"I haven't finished explaining the whole thing to you as yet," I broke in without letting him finish. "As we told you, we need the department's staff to generate the growth of the plants and the imprinting of the Macrosoft logo on their leaves. Because of the impact we want to make, everything must happen very, very fast and very effectively so that the effect will be astonishing. However, even though I know that this is the basis of our campaign, I'm not sure whether the effect will be sufficiently emotional, and this is where you come in as a production expert. What could we do to touch the hearts of the people who see the campaign? How can we generate an image they won't forget? Are the plants enough?"

"Do you want me to produce an emotional campaign?" he said, raising his emotion-filled eyes again.

"Yes, but remember that the budget is limited."

"I've spent so long looking for a campaign with heart that I'm not sure I'm able. I don't think I have a heart."

"Timothy, everybody has a heart. Don't forget that it's the only organ that keeps on working, no matter how cold and broken it is. Can I tell you a story?"

"A story?" Oscar looked surprised.

"Yes, a very important person showed me that by using familiar language and metaphor, ideas make themselves understood and lessons are better remembered. And I've just remembered a perfect story for this situation."

Oscar made a gesture to show that he was in favour, while Tim leaned forward over his desk with his eyes full of curiosity.

I thought for a moment, and then began the story.

> "When I first met Antoine Bellagio and Amelie Bèrger I thought they were an amazing couple. He was a crazy dreamer and she was a respectable Parisian scientist. He was a hopeless practical joker, and she was his most faithful fan and follower. Nobody had every heard them have an argument in forty years of married life. They empathised with each other, understood each other and respected each other above all. Each always had time for the other, always time to talk.
>
> "They used to like strolling through the Champs-Élysées, visiting the most hidden corners of Montmartre or enjoying watching the couples who swarmed around the Eiffel

Tower, taking the standard souvenir photos. They loved to walk hand-in-hand when the streets were flooded with that lovely smell of fresh bread in the early morning. And even then, they were always talking.

"A friend told me that the secret was that Antoine was in love with Amelie to the depths of her being, but there was one part of her where he was completely vulnerable, and to which he was truly devoted. It was her voice.

"Whenever he felt nervous, it was Amelie's voice which calmed him down. When he was exhausted, it gave him energy, even when he was away or travelling for his work, he needed to Amelie's voce to keep going.

"The tragedy happened. Amelie died of a terrible illness just two years ago. But just before she died, knowing how he felt, she handed a leather bag to her beloved, telling him that he was only to open it in an extreme emergency. That night they talked for hours until Amelie's flame flickered and went out. Antoine burst into tears, clutching the leather bag.

"Nobody could do anything for such awful grief, and as the days passed his physical condition began to deteriorate. He felt his heart was in rags, torn from his body, weak, sad. A cloud of nothingness surrounded him, and where in the past there had been smiles, now the furrows on his face revealed his utter loneliness.

"One morning as he was walking through the park towards his house he began to feel that he could stand it no longer, and he fell to the ground. His eyes closed, his heart slowly stopped and he began to grow cold.

"A young man who was jogging nearby ran to help him and tried unsuccessfully to resuscitate him, although it seemed that Antoine didn't want to come back to life because of his own will. After a few minutes, desperate, the young man decided that it was a heart attack, and that there should be some tablets nearby. He looked in his pockets, and finding nothing, noticed the leather bag and opened it.

It was just at that moment, when he tugged at the cords which closed the bag and looked inside that a sigh seemed to emerge from it. It was Amelie's voice softly whispering a sentence which the young man could not understand. Bemused, he looked back at Antoine and he was able to see that although Antoine was still lying on the ground, he was smiling broadly."

I finished the story and noticed that Tim's eyes were moist. Oscar, looking amazed, couldn't wait for the punch line and asked:

"What was she saying?"

"Yes Dorothy, what was she saying?" Tim was also asking.

"Whatever it was, it isn't important. What is important is that Tim, as we can clearly see, has not lost the ability to be moved, that his heart is still alive. When you hear that song that moves you, when you read that story that does something to you, even when Mrs. West drives you crazy, you are experiencing emotion. You're alive, Tim, and the ability to feel is in all of us. It may be that some people are losing the ability to show their feelings, or even to empathise with others problems, but they cannot lose the ability to feel."

"Obviously I have feelings, Dorothy, but how can I do anything that has an emotional content?"

"Look inside yourself, look for the roots of the feelings and try to make others feel the same way. Get your colleagues to share whatever it is that moves your heart, and get interested in their emotions. That would be a good start."

Tim read the notes he had written for a moment or two, together with the documentation on the campaign we had brought him.

"It's time to go to work! I accept the challenge, Dorothy."

"I knew you'd do it." Our eyes met.

We got up, and as we moved towards the door we could hear Tim calling to his secretary.

"Anna, could you call the team together for a meeting, please?"

"Of course, Mr. Mann. What would be the reason for the meeting?"

"Reason? No reason," he said, giving us a conspiratorial glance, "I just want to take some time out to talk."

Before we left, in the purest of Henry styles, I turned to him as he held the door and said:

" 'I missed your smile'." I winked. "That was the sentence which Amelie put into the leather bag."

8

Lionel Kövard

"Wherever you find a successful business,
you'll find someone taking courageous decisions"

Peter Drucker

When I got back to my office my face was wreathed in a smile of satisfaction. Oscar, who had got out of the lift on floor seventeen, wanted to carry out a few tests, to check that everything was perfectly synchronised and that the plants were reacting correctly to the vitamin treatment. He also said that he would take the opportunity to tell his departmental colleagues how the project was proceeding, since now that he had decided that it would succeed, he wanted it to be a success for everybody.

There was no doubt that everything was working perfectly, but I could not allow myself to relax. I had to keep working on the campaign. This project involved much more than the outcome of a client's account. It was the perfect opportunity to show Heidi and Henry that they had been right to choose me for the job.

I thought for a moment about Henry and remembered the last conversation I had had with him about Mrs. West. That particular lady's intentions were far from clear, so, since all members of the team were in position and had begun to work, I decided to give him a call. The telephone rang several times, but since he seemed not to be answering I decided to send him an email. I spent over two hours writing, deleting and then re-writing, and the final message looked like this:

> *Dear Henry,*
>
> *How is everything going? I imagine that the arrival of spring in Kansas is really lighting up the parks and avenues, as it always does.*
>
> *I'm writing to tell you that I'm currently working on the campaign for Macrosoft's new operating system. One thing I can tell you is that Oscar Crow, the Research Department manager, and Timothy Mann, Head of Production, have turned out to be great discoveries. I'm really looking forward to seeing the results of their talent.*
>
> *On another completely different subject, how are the negotiations going with Mrs. West? Has she made you any offers? Did you manage to postpone the meeting? I would really like to know what her actual interest in the situation is.*
>
> *In closing, I have to thank you for the stories you told me over so many years and the unique way you taught me to be a real professional. At the present moment I am getting a very great deal out of your tales. Now I understand how much pleasure it must have given you to see me finding out the solutions.*
>
> *That really is about all for now, Uncle Henry, so I'll sign off by saying that I'm looking forward to your news.*
>
> *Big hugs,*
>
> *Dorothy*

I was just about to check that the email had arrived, but even as my finger hovered over the key…

"Dorothy, there's a call for you on the inside line."

"Thanks, Boq… Hello, what's happening?"

"Dorothy, I think I've found the solution."

It was Tim, and he sounded very excited. He started to tell me how he had worked out where he could get the extra material for our campaign. The way he explained it was full of passion and enthusiasm, colouring in all the details as though he could see them before his eyes. In fact, if you closed your eyes it was as though you could touch the result. He was talking to me about sensations, colours, and emotions. I let him talk for a while, then asked him the unavoidable question.

"It sounds fantastic, Tim, but… How can we possibly do it? It will cost a fortune."

"But that's the best part about it. You see, last year I had the opportunity to spend some time on a leadership course held at a nearby farm where the same problem came up. What it comes down to is that they would even be willing to pay to get rid of their surplus crop. So relax – I'm head of production, right? Let me be responsible for assessing availability and checking out if we really can make use of these plants."

"Brilliant, I'll call Oscar to check on the compatibility of the plants and to tell him all about your idea. How does that sound?"

"Perfect. We must all be kept abreast of all incoming information so that we can manage it the best way possible. I'll give you a call directly and let you know what progress I've made."

"Thanks for that, we'll talk later."

The idea was brilliant, and a warm feeling suffused my body as I dialled Oscar's number. I could hardly believe that such an emotional concept could have been created by someone who had been telling me he didn't have a heart only a few hours ago.

"Hi, Dorothy. The tests have all been successful. How are things at your end?"

I started explaining Tim's idea to him, including all the details, just as he had put it to me. I told him about the farm, the colours, the additional plants, everything.

"Congratulations! This is going to be a campaign that will be remembered for a long time. I'm really proud to be involved in the project. As regards the compatibility of the two ideas, I can't see any problem – this was one of the things we had to test when we started the plant research programme."

"Many thanks, Oscar, but this is a team project in the widest meaning of the word. And, yes, I'm in full agreement with you that if we can pull this off, it really will be memorable – well, that's what the client wants, right?"

"You're right there! So now there's just one detail missing, the communications department. They must really pull out all the stops to optimise resources, because otherwise we're going to go outside the budget, and that really would be a pity."

"Take it easy, Oscar, it'll be okay. Who is the head of communications?"

"His name's Lionel Kövard. Would you like me come with you to meet with him tomorrow?"

"Let's wait to see what Tim has to say about his idea, and once we've got that side of things settled all three of us can go and explain to him exactly what the idea consists of. Does that sound okay?"

"Great, Dorothy. I'll wait for your call."

When I rang off I remembered something very important about team management which lodged in my head while I was watching the Japan 2006 basketball semi-finals. After the match, and unexpected Greek victory over the unbeatable USA team, Theodoros Papaloukas, one of the Greek selection members, said: "We may not be such great athletes as them but we play as a team. Jumping higher and running faster isn't always the key to victory. This is a team sport, not tennis".

When he said that he was obviously talking about the synergy of working teams, the way in which the integration of all the elements gives rise to something greater than the simple sum of those elements, like the parts of an aeroplane, for example. Individually the parts are unable to fly, but when you put them together they can move at incredible speeds. In the same way the hands of a watch alone can't tell us what time it is – they need the internal mechanism.

I felt proud to be able to say that I was creating a synergetic team. Each individual contributed a crucial input, and the result was beginning to appear. Then the unmistakable sound of the in-tray told me that an email had arrived while I was musing.

Hi, Freckles,

I was delighted to read your email and to hear that everything is going so well. Macrosoft is going to be proud of your work.

Everything is going well down here on the Farm. There's plenty of work, as usual, but no-body complains about that, right?

As regards my meeting with Oz Company, this has finally been settled for three weeks time, the first week of May, to be precise. They have now explained to us their intention to try to find state-based part-ners with a view to set-ting up a huge, world-wide marketing group. It certainly sounds fantastic.

I hope to be able to get a moment to give you a call in the next few days so I can tell you more.

A big hug,
Henry Baum

P.S. Once you've found your tigon, don't forget to house-train it.

What an amazing man. Even over the internet he could calm down a situation which was giving me increasingly bad vibes, and even more so since Boq described the way companies were being taken over. My lower lip was starting to feel the force of my teeth again.

"Dorothy, excuse me again, but you have Timothy Mann on line one."

"Hi, Tim. What's the news?"

"It's even better than I thought! Do you remember that I told you that the farms had to get rid of their surplus product? Well, it seems that this is a widespread problem for farms in this sector. We can count on maybe one hundred times as many plants as we originally thought. And the best of it is that it will cost us only about fifteen thousand dollars for transportation."

"What? Can we really get our hands on half a million plants? Close the deal immediately and we'll have a meeting in an hour with the staff of all three departments so that everybody will understand the details of the operation. Agreed?"

"You've got it. I still can't believe it – this is going to be fantastic!"

"It's going to be better than that. And Tim, I can't thank you enough for your wonderful work!"

Laughs, smiles of understanding, handshakes. That was what you saw when all the details had been explained to our team. No-one could believe that we could have come up with such a concept.

"No, it's everybody's creation – we're a team, and as you know, greatness lies in simple ideas. We're on a very good track here."

"All that remains is for the idea to keep thriving and to be communicated perfectly," Tim answered.

"Precisely, and for that we have to have the communications department in on it," I said, turning towards Oscar.

"That's right, Dorothy, we must have a meeting with Lionel."

"Okay, listen everybody," I faced my colleagues, "this is our task, a big project which must have an impact and work. Tim, Oscar and I will have a meeting with Lionel and the communications department while you carry on with your jobs to the best of your ability. I trust you, I trust your work and your abilities. You've all got the instructions in the report. But there's just one more thing I have to ask of you: maintain the element of surprise. This has to be kept a secret from everybody, because that's the only way we can reach people's hearts. Good luck!"

Spontaneously everybody started to talk with the members of the other departments with which they had to coordinate. The company was coming to life.

Tim, Oscar and I made ready for the meeting on the next day with Lionel Kövard. Obviously, I had to ask them about him.

It turned out that Lionel was a dynamic young Swede who had been hired by Oz Company in the wake of his amazing successes for a huge furniture company. He was very friendly, with highly developed social skills. My friends described him as approachable, easy-going, smart and determined. It looked as though working with him would be enriching and easy. At least, so I thought.

9

The Road to Excellence

> *"He who has never faced adversity does*
> *not know his own strength"*
>
> *Benjamin Jonson*

During the night I went over the idea a few more times in my mind as preparation as it was really important to convince our communications department, to ensure that they had credibility and trust. Obviously, all the pieces had to fit together perfectly, and that meant that the part to be played by communications was crucial for the final stage.

Tim and Oscar were speaking on their cell phones to their respective secretaries, organising their schedules, as we went up in the lift to floor thirty. A sign told us that this was the department of communications and public relations. As we walked into the office I noticed to my surprise that the white image adopted by the company had been subtly changed. Scores of plants covered the shelves, amazing photographs of animals adorned the staff tables and furniture, and high quality timber and ergonomic chairs gave the room a very natural feel.

"Welcome to my little jungle," Lionel said as he came to meet us.

Lionel Kövard was a good-looking young man. Penetrating honey-coloured eyes and a blond, rather frizzy, mop of hair were the first physical things you noticed. His huge smile and carefully manicured hands indicated that he was certainly endowed with social skills.

"Hey, Oscar, long time no see! How is the research proceeding? I'm itching to communicate the progress you're making on the new laser screens."

"Well, I can tell you that we're certainly on the right track. I hope to be starting with some saleable results very soon."

"I'm delighted to hear it. And how about you, Timothy? Let me congratulate you on the recent campaigns. The production of television promotion initiatives was excellent."

"Thanks, Lionel. The previous work was very good, all we did was what they told us to do."

"You're too modest. Your work is always exact and effective, which is really important for a company such as ours. So, lady and gentlemen, how can I be of service to you and the new creative manager?"

"I'm Dorothy Grimm, pleased to meet you," I said amicably.

"The pleasure is mine. I'm not used to such a collection of talent in my office."

"Thanks again. Well, the situation is this, Lionel. We've designed a new campaign for Macrosoft and we need your help to communicate it effectively, both to the client and to the public."

"Well, you've come to the right place. Tell me what it's all about," he said with a huge smile. "But let's go and sit down in the centre there. We'll be more comfortable."

As soon as we were seated I began to explain to him all the details of the campaign. The expression on his face was that of a child on his birthday. He investigated the specifics to see if everything matched, checked effectiveness, and as he followed the whole story he examined every aspect to make sure that there were no cracks.

"This is brilliant, and it'll be a big success for Oz Company. Just one more question. What caused you to end up creating something like this?"

"I suppose you could say that necessity is the mother of invention," I grinned.

"Necessity?"

"Well, you can imagine, when I started to consider a campaign for Macrosoft I was planning on a huge media project, with adverts on different supports and a high impact television ad, dripping with aesthetics as well as message. However, when the finance department started to raise economic problems we found ourselves obliged to think again."

"So Mrs. West is not in agreement?" His face had changed.

"I can't hide the fact that an unfortunate episode occurred on my first day at the office and I guess I would have to say that I'm unlikely to be found on the list of her best friends," I said, trying to make light of it.

"Dorothy, I would love to help you, but alas, unfortunately I am in no position to do so," he said, getting up.

Lionel's face had gone rigid. His frightened expression and hesitant voice conveyed to me the extent of the contradictory feelings he was experiencing.

"What's the matter, Lionel, what are you talking about?" Oscar quickly asked.

"That's all there is to it. I can't help you."

"But you're the head of communications. If you aren't, then who is?" Tim cut in rather sharply.

"I'm not joking, I just can't. The idea is brilliant, but under the circumstances I'm unable to help you with the communication. I'll send one of my staff tomorrow to begin the usual process."

"What did you mean, you can't? You can if you want to," Tim pressed.

"It isn't like that… you don't understand" he said, fixing me with a look that seemed to beg forgiveness.

"Let's all stay calm," I said smoothly. "What is it that we have to understand?

"If I help you, I shall have to confront Mrs. West. And of that I am truly scared. She has more power than anyone else at Oz Company and she will not hesitate to use it against me if she knows that I am involved in this project," he excused himself. "Just try to understand."

"Listen, Lionel, you're just the same as us. You're doing your job in the best way you can, so there's no way the company can cause you problems, right?"

"The company can't, but she can…"

"What is it that most scares you about her? Are you afraid to face Mrs. West?"

"I'm afraid of losing my job." He put his head in his hands.

"And you think that if you do your job correctly you can lose it?"

"It's not that, it's just that Mrs. West knows how to use information and she works the investors any way she wants. I joined the company after she personally made life impossible for my predecessor and the whole department. They would never forgive me. They were very difficult months for my colleagues."

"So which are you afraid of? Losing your job or generating ill-feeling among your colleagues?"

"I suppose it's both." He was trying to get me to understand.

"Okay, Lionel, let's take it step by step. Why did Oz Company hire you?"

"I guess it's because they thought I was right for the position. I presume they think I'm good."

"Do you think that, or know it?" I asked.

"It doesn't look very modest if I say I am good, does it?"

"Okay, you don't want to say it, let's look at the facts. How many campaigns have you developed for Oz Company?"

"Almost fifty," he replied proudly.

"Fine. How many of those fifty could be seen as a failure or as having a negative side for the client?"

"A failure? Not one, although I suppose there's always room for improvement."

"How many prizes have you been awarded for your past work?"

"I got the Golden Lion at the Cannes Advertising Festival, and I've been highly recommended three times by El Sol, the Latin American Advertising Communication Festival."

"Have you won any prizes since you've been with Oz?"

"I've received two more Sol prizes and a 'Dummy', the prize for the Children's Advertising Festival, over these two years."

"In other words, if we try to be objective, we could say that you're among the elite of advertising communicators, right?"

"Well, I suppose you could see it like that… but it isn't just my work, I've got a fantastic team backing me," he tried to make excuses.

"What does the knowledge that you have a fantastic team behind you give you?"

"Peace of mind, strength, energy, motivation… but where are you going with this, Dorothy?"

"To this exact moment."

"I don't understand." He raised his perfect, blond eyebrows.

"I have news for you, Lionel. If you carry on clinging to your fear you'll never achieve anything, and the strange thing is that you have no reason to keep clinging to it. The only way you can overcome your fears is by facing them. But, of course, to do that you need to know that the resources you can count on are good enough. In other words, if, for example, you're afraid of heights, you could try sky diving to get over it, but first you must check that the pilot has a licence, that the parachute is ready for use, and that the instructor who jumps with you has the necessary experience. Understand?"

"Yes, but I still don't really know..." He looked confused.

"It's very easy. We know that you're a success, because you win international prizes. We know that you're doing excellent work because, of the fifty campaigns you have run with Oz, not one has made a false step. And we know that you're a team player, and that if you have a powerful team you feel at ease, powerful and motivated."

I waited a couple of seconds, engaged eye contact, put out my hand and said: "Hi, I'm Dorothy Grimm, manager of the creative department of Oz Company, and I would like to communicate to you that my friends and I are with you, we believe in you and we are completely confident that you are going to do an excellent job."

"Thank you, Dorothy," he said, blushing.

"Hi, my name's Oscar Crow, manager of the research and development department. You know that I've always helped you and I will continue to do so, because I believe in your potential and your ability." Oscar continued as he held out his hand, "My team is at your service."

"Hi, my name is Timothy Mann, manager of the production department. Each and every one of my team are right behind you. We know that our work is always effectively sold because of the communication work you do."

Lionel was smiling and his rather misty eyes moved from one of our faces to another. He appeared to be deeply moved.

"Thank you, you're wonderful."

"No thanks are needed, this is just what you get for your work. Now, let's get rid of these fears. The first thing you're scared of is losing your job. As you can see, nobody in their right mind would ever risk having to do without a talent like yours. But even if it were to happen, could you imagine that someone with your CV and skills would have to spend much time looking for another similar position?"

"Well, I guess not, in fact I do get offers every now and again."

"So this is not really a problem, right?"

"It really isn't," he agreed with certainty.

"Okay. Now let's talk about your team and Mrs. West. As you can see, we are three members of the management who support you, and we also have the backing of Miss Heidi North. Mrs. West has implemented a policy based on fear in this company, and so far, perhaps because people feel isolated or perhaps because of the survival instinct, no-one has faced up to her. That has now come to an end. I for one will not permit my team to be ill-treated because of some whimsical decision of hers. And if it turns out that I'm required to come up with original ideas such as this, requiring the coordination of the various departments in the company, I shall have to carry on doing so."

"Well said, Dorothy," added Tim. "My thinking is exactly the same as our young redhead here. I, too, want to generate change, and if that means injecting some heart into the production department and creating more emotional products, then that is what I shall do."

"That goes for me, too," continued Oscar. "The research and development department has been sleep walking for months, but now we're awake again. Big changes start with small actions. So if making big changes here at Oz means developing more creative and brilliant ideas, then I'll do it."

Lionel studied us for a few seconds and then said:

"You know what? You're right. My team trusts me and I keep the peace for them, but on condition that I give up our ideas. The time has come for me to find the necessary courage to change this company back to what it really used to be and what it never should have ceased to be. The time to face our responsibilities has come."

At that very moment we all felt that something had changed within us. The seed of commitment had germinated, and now was the time to water it and fertilise it so that it could grow into a big strong tree.

"Right. Then just run through the details one more time for me, so that we can set to work," Lionel insisted.

Once again we explained the whole project to him, step by step. But just before we could finish we were interrupted.

"Well, well. So the sheep are having a meeting..."

It was Mrs. West. She was wearing a brilliant green suit of excellent cut which showed off her magnificent figure. Emerald green high-heel shoes clicked on the hardwood floor. Impeccable makeup in greenish tones illuminated and enhanced the great power in her eyes.

"Dorothy, my dear, how is the Macrosoft campaign proceeding? I trust you have no problems in that regard."

"None whatever, our ideas are taking shape even as we speak, and very soon we'll be able to present it to the client. I'll pass expenses over to you with the final budget, which will be adjusted to the budget initially allotted by the financial department," I answered with a sarcastic tone.

"I look forward to that. By the way, I should like to be there when you make the presentation to the client. I imagine you will have no problem with that?"

"I'm absolutely certain that won't be necessary, although I'm grateful for your offer. The meeting will be for the heads of the departments concerned with creating and developing the campaign. But don't worry, we'll keep you informed about how the project proceeds."

I am unable to describe the fury which she concealed behind her perfect, chiselled smile.

"I'm afraid I must insist. I really would like to be there," she hissed.

"I'm very sorry, Mrs. West, but the decision has been taken. Timothy will produce the campaign and will have to explain the details. Oscar will not be making available obsolete material regarding the campaign for Oz Company, but material which is very advanced and innovative. I would be unable to explain matters to the client if he were to ask me about it. And, naturally, Lionel will be in charge of the communication aspects and the media plan. No-one is better qualified than him to explain the procedure to Macrosoft. The people who must be there, will be there, and additional individuals will only confuse the client. It may also turn out that the company is not fully confident in us and may feel that someone must be instructed to supervise our work, and if that were to happen, obviously it would be a disaster if such information were to reach the ears of our investors, wouldn't it?"

Her eyes were like two burning pits of fire with green sparks, but the smile remained in place, and she went on:

"Very well, Dorothy, I see that you have it all worked out. I'm delighted to see that the campaign is in such good hands. But there is one matter which needs to be set right. I was on my way to inform Lionel that he needs to prioritise and get to work on our next annual general meeting. I know that there are still three months to go, but something tells me that the most important piece of news to affect Oz Company since the company was founded is going to be announced. This means that all our advertisers, clients and partners must be mobilised, along with the communications media. Everybody must be there."

10

A Little Magic

"What is surprising is surprising once only.
What is admirable is always so"

Joseph Joubert

Lionel had to work hard over the next few days. Keeping Mrs. West happy after our meeting was far from easy, but thanks to the support of his team not only was he able to prepare the meeting, but he was also able to work out something really fantastic for our campaign. I had to work hard over the next few days also.

Over those days we had meetings with the client, and we demanded absolute secrecy from him. Markus Mark, the Macrosoft President, congratulated us and applauded such a fabulous idea. In the end we decided on our key day for the launch of the project as the first of May. We had three weeks to prepare for the big day. But before that happened we had to create an atmosphere of expectation.

I had a meeting with Boq, the viral marketing expert, to talk about generating a feeling of excitement, of anticipation, getting everybody talking about it. However, since we were short of cash, despite the fact that we had saved a lot thanks to the contributions made by Oscar and Tim, we decided that we ourselves would appear on the promotional videos.

I remember that in my video the screen was orange with the phrase "A little magic" appearing on it. The camera then picked up my amazed face as I looked out of a window at something I found hard to believe. The opening colours of the advertisements separately showed the Macrosoft colours. To make it come alive we got out some of our colleagues dressed as firemen and police performing their duties and also revealing the same look of amazement. With two of them we managed to appear on all the virus pages, including the TV programmes which broadcast sections of other TV programmes, what are known as zapping programmes. One of the adverts showed what was supposed to be the President of the USA playing sudoku, and another a female couple having sex. It was a hit. Everyone was talking about whoever it could be behind it, since most people guessed that it had to be a marketing campaign. What was best of all was that producing and broadcasting the videos cost barely twenty-two thousand dollars.

On April fifteen we went public. Macrosoft was to donate to the city of New York the incredible number of one thousand beautiful plants, each almost two metres in height, to beautify the parks and main avenues. The donation was explained as an environmental commitment on the part of the company, an aspect of their well-known corporate social responsibility. The media had a field day, economic analysts praised the company's approach and encouraged other market leaders to imitate the gesture.

That day I got a call from Lionel.

"What do you think?"

"Brilliant, even today's newspapers are full of it. How did you pull it off?"

"It wasn't hard. The news media have their patterns, and although hundreds of different news items come up every day, the media make their choices according to whatever the editorial line for that day may be. For example, if you want to pressurise the government about fuel prices, you choose items about wars in OPEC countries, market fluctuations, indirect taxation and so on."

"I get it."

"Following this line of action, corporate social responsibility is currently very fashionable. People feel that they have a right to force large companies to give something back to society in some way or other in the way of social action. But almost all these actions end up in the third world, or at least at a great distance from the citizen."

"I see. But this is quite different. All of the citizens of New York can enjoy these plants in their city, right?"

"Sure. It's something tangible and the people like it. Everybody wants to be involved. What's more, since Macrosoft is to be found everywhere in the world the excitement has spread world-wide in a matter of hours."

"There's a lesson in this, Lionel, that we have to make the most of all the resources at our disposal and use this terrible globalisation to our own advantage."

"I couldn't have put it better myself. Still, now we have stage two to deal with, and I can't wait for the day to come. The press wants to see the talk to be given by the president of the company, which will happen on the same day as the planting."

"Has the competition started to react?"

"Of course, all day long they're putting out press releases watering down the action and spreading the word that it's all a publicity stunt to cover the launch of the new product. The communications media will soon start to parrot them."

"But that's perfect. They have taken over the job of spreading the word that the new operating system is about to come on sale. In other words, they're running our campaign for us free of charge. Mrs. West must be delighted," I joked.

"This is just what we wanted. They and their commentaries will do the work of selling and discussing the technical side of our client, leaving us responsible for the commitment and support messages."

"We still have the final fireworks," he said excitedly.

"I really want to see it all!" I chorused back.

We spent a few moments talking about how things were going and finally I hung up, unable to contain a little cheer. My colleagues began to laugh at me and make signs that they were with me. Everything was working.

Everything happened so fast that the night before the big day I could hardly sleep. The encouraging messages from all my colleagues, the final tests on the preparations and the anticipation were pounding inside my head. I really had to calm down or I was going to make my appearance with serious bags under my eyes. In the end, after a bit of tossing and turning, I finally went to sleep.

Wednesday, May the first. From early in the morning the streets and parks of the city had been filling up with people. It was a holiday, so everybody was making the most of the first rays of the sun and of the rising temperature to enjoy a day in the open air. And here I was, strolling down Fifth Avenue in the direction of Central Park. This was a special day, so I had dressed for the occasion. I was wearing a fantastic chocolate and red suit, I had my hair down and just a touch of earth tone makeup as accessories to my great treasure – the red Mugatu shoes. They were really unbelievably beautiful, but what was the biggest surprise was how comfortable they were to walk in. Each step made me feel more powerful, braver, more ready.

When I reached our chosen area, Tim was waiting for me.

"Wow, Ginger, you look great! And the shoes are really fabulous."

"Thanks. Tim, and that is one great suit!" I returned his compliment.

"Thank you. Okay, here's the situation. The stand is ready, and the PA system. Everything is ready to start at eleven in the morning, that's to say, barely two hours from now. The Mayor of New York will offer his thanks for the company's gesture and will make a speech to the people wishing them a great day, and hoping they all have fun. The President takes over, talking about corporate responsibility and the commitment made by all the people who have made Macrosoft into the great company it is today. At a maximum that should last about half an hour. Oscar has everything ready and his people and mine have been busy all night preparing the fabulous plants together with the workers which city hall has been kind enough to lend us. Lionel called the press half an hour ago and stressed the fact that the general news agencies should be there with video cameras. They'll meet with us in an hour, when everything is ready."

"Perfect, Tim. Would you ask Heidi North to give the staff a few days off until next Monday? When all is said and done they can be seen as working days that they can tack onto the weekend to get some rest. The effort they've put in over these weeks deserves at least that. And let me congratulate you on a magnificent job of work."

"Great idea, I'll talk to Heidi. And you're right, Dorothy, everybody has put in the work. Now we just cross our fingers and pray for good luck."

"No, Tim," I disagreed, "let's leave luck for when we need it. We've put in the work and taken care of all the details. We created the opportunity and ironed out all the possible problems. Believe me, we don't need any luck today."

I did experience a small shiver of nerves, I have to admit, but I wanted all my colleagues to see me as sure and confident. My lower lip might have given me away, but I made every effort to make sure that my teeth gave up the habit of biting my lip for once. I needed them one hundred per cent. I was not going to let my uncertainty fill me with absurd fears which would be communicated to them.

At the appointed time the news media started to show up. We gave them a warm reception and a dazed Lionel greeted them one by one. Some joked:

"Hey, they're making us work on a holiday…"

"This moment will be remembered for quite a while, and you're gong to be witnesses to it in person. I feel sorry for the people who'll only be able to see this on the TV." He smiled broadly at them.

"Lionel, the only reason we're here is to cover the news of the Macrosoft gesture and the Mayor's speech. I don't think that's going to be so exciting," said one humorous cameraman.

"Don't take anything for granted, Roger, I can assure you there is one big surprise waiting at the end. Something you've never seen in your life."

The journalists pressed him with questions, but he made a move like someone zipping up and locking his lips. Just a few moments later Tim and Oscar called us to take our seats in the second row. The die was cast.

Mrs. West, impeccably dressed in carmine, looked me up and down, and as we took our seats, she said.

"Well, maybe you aren't a completely lost cause as far as taste is concerned. Those shoes certainly look fabulous."

"Well… thank you."

Her friendliness was confusing, but I felt I had to give my whole attention to the action that was starting to take place. Marcus Mark, seated on the front row, turned to me and said:

"Whatever happens, you have my gratitude. These last few days have been fun, so full of excitement and enthusiasm."

Clapping burst out all over Central Park, as the Mayor opened the proceedings. The stage was a large space decorated with the Macrosoft corporate colours: orange, green, blue and yellow. Two horizontal banners bore the legend "A little magic", a reference to the famous viral campaign. The base of the stage was a huge screen showing, in the wake of some nature-type images, an initial shot of the Mayor. Above the stage, one of the plants symbolised the action.

After an emotional, rather sentimental speech which included terms such as commitment, responsibility and efficiency, and which made it clear that the company had always been at the cutting edge of technology, making life easier for people, the master of ceremonies introduced the company President.

"First, let me wish you all a really great and happy day," he began, and Timothy took out his mobile phone to make a call.

"This is the moment," he said.

Hanging up, he looked at me and smiled. Three minutes later the President uttered the key words. "A company which wishes to be a leader must always give priority to people. And now more than ever it must respect and collaborate in the fight against climate change. Other ways are possible, at least I dream that they are. As everybody knows, I've spent years transforming my dreams and those of millions of others into reality. Surely we can accomplish this?"

At that moment the President picked up a watering can and watered the plant on the stage. The municipal workers, primed by the staff of the research and development section, did the same to the thousand plants distributed throughout the city.

People were on the point of applauding the gesture, but it was only seconds later that the magic appeared. A perfect Macrosoft logo rapidly appeared on the leaves of the plant on the stage. To make it all the more appropriate, we had chosen the logo with the butterfly which the brand used to use a few years back. The TV cameras, which at this moment were recording the first cut of the watering, were dumbstruck, giving full seconds of time in the news flashes to our client. An incredible exclamation of amazement spread from the stage to the furthest corners of Central Park. People came up to the plants to touch them. They couldn't believe their eyes. And just at the moment when the flower which appeared at the top of the plants was beginning to open, Oscar turned to me and I said:

"There's your brain. Not only were you enough of a visionary to create something as wonderful as this, you also knew how to go back to and use those resources afresh when you needed them."

Oscar, moved by the indirect applause, gave me a wink and stared at the sky. A strange sound began to be heard, a powerful breathing, like the waves on the sea, beating again and again, and at every beat it came nearer. Suddenly thousands of orange butterflies began to appear in the great avenues, between the parked cars, even between the huge glass buildings which surrounded the handsome park, attracted by the flowers and their pollen. Then, thousand of blue butterflies appeared, flying over the huge lake, packed with people. The spectacle grew in intensity at the same rate as the amazement of the people witnessing the event, of the journalists, and even of each and every one of us who had taken part in the event when the green and yellow butterflies filled the sky in a sea of colour reminiscent of the famous brand logo.

Hundreds of thousands of butterflies fluttered through the sky alternating the colours and creating optical illusions worthy of the best of Hollywood's effects. Everything was flooded by those beautiful creatures in danger of extinction which are now, due to new and successful breeding programmes, creating a super-population in their breeding farms. The unequalled visual display was simply spectacular.

"And there is your heart. You have been able to create a fascinating emotion in hundreds of thousands of people. You complied with the standards, but you were able to empathise and fill hearts with excitement," I said to Tim as he fought with his tears.

The President returned to the microphone and concluded.

"It is nature which provides us with these scenes of unparalleled beauty. It cares for us and provides us with everything we need. Now is the time for us to return, at the least a little, of what we have been given. Thank you."

The applause was deafening. The staff from our departments were embracing each other, celebrating the success, the Macrosoft staff congratulated each other and cheered. Some had tears in their eyes as they gazed at the Oz Company managers. Markus turned around and, unable to contain himself, embraced me and said once again: "Congratulations".

The journalists, completely concentrated on the story, were making phone calls to explain what they were seeing to their editorial staff. Some of the television networks could show live coverage, and they continued to shoot more and more footage to immortalise this magic moment.

"There's your courage," I smiled at Lionel. "You were able to make use of the resources that the market offered you and not to discard the possibilities. You confronted your fears and the result will be recorded and communicated to the four corners of the earth, thanks to your courage."

Lionel rose, kissed me on the cheek, said "Thanks for sharing this success with me" and headed off to attend to the press contingent.

His task was not yet at an end, since now he had to explain to the citizens that this was not merely an advertising campaign, and that the marks on the leaves would disappear in around four weeks. It was also important to point out that, thanks to the wisdom of nature, the butterflies would slowly spread out to cover the whole country, thus meeting the pressing need for repopulation.

Just for a few moments I looked around me, enjoying that wonderful scene. It was fantastic, everything had turned out perfectly. Thousands of leaves with our client's logo, hundreds of thousands of butterflies reproducing his corporate colours in an action which would be fixed in everybody's heart, and, of course, the millions of smiles on peoples' lips told me in a tangible way that the campaign had been a success.

Before I slipped away to celebrate with my colleagues, I remembered the famous advertisement for credit cards.

> "Transporting half a million butterflies, fifteen thousand dollars. Creating viral marketing videos, twenty-two thousand dollars. Setting up a wonderful stage, eighty-three thousand dollars. Seeing Mrs. West's face as she explained who had been responsible for this campaign – priceless".

11

Choosing the Road to Oz

"If inspiration doesn't come to me
I go out and meet it half way"

Sigmund Freud

Over the weekend I received hundreds of emails congratulating me. The news media talked about it endlessly, all including spectacular images. The newspapers coloured their usually black and white pages with excellent photographs of the flight of the butterflies and of the plants displaying the logo. Advertising that you could not buy for our client, and a moment that would be fixed in our memories for years, one which it would be very difficult to better.

In particular there were two messages which I valued more than most. The first was important because of the professional aspect and the recognition implicit in it.

Dear Dorothy Grimm,

Allow us to congratulate you for the excellent job you did for Macrosoft, a campaign full of life, totally original and with amazing impact. I wish you many more successes and I hope to be able to work with you some time in the future.

S. Jobs
Director,
Mapple

The second was more important because of the emotional content.

Dear Freckles,

Today you graduated from the University of the World with honours. Thank you for the thrill you gave me and for your generosity in sharing your talent with me.

You will receive many prizes, thanks to which we will be able to relive that Wednesday. It's been years since this sector was revolutionised, and it took you to do it.

I look forward to enjoying your campaigns for a long time to come.

A warm embrace from your friend and admirer,

Henry Baum

P.S. The meeting takes place next Tuesday, May the seventh. I'll keep you informed.

If anyone could have stopped time at that moment and measured the happiness of everyone in the world, there is no doubt I should have come out ahead. All I wanted to do was to enjoy it and wait for the good times and the smiles of my friends in the office on Monday.

However, on the first day of the week I received chilling and disturbing news; unexpected, too, and extremely worrying. While some newspapers were still talking about last Wednesday's event, the corporate website and some radio stations were beginning to pick up the news: Oz Company was taking over a number of companies in several states, thus becoming the largest marketing business in the country.

Mrs. West had played her cards well, and, taking advantage of the fame and good management of the Macrosoft campaign, had convinced the investors to make the financial effort for the operation. I wasn't bothered about the fact that she had bypassed my little moment of glory; what concerned me was the situation down on the Farm, since now there was no secret to be kept, and the policy and strategy were out in the open. I had to prevent Oz from buying the Kansas company, because if things went otherwise I could never forgive myself for the fact that it was my success that allowed Mrs. West to get the support she needed to sideline Henry.

But bad news never comes alone. An email arrived marked urgent which left me frozen. It had been addressed to all Oz management and investors.

Dear friend and colleague,

As you know the business is at present enjoying great success thanks to the work that has been put in by each and every one of the teams and the excellent management system which is being put in place at the finance department.

This management system has resulted in our being the leading marketing company in the country and means that we are one of the most profitable companies in this sector in the world.

In addition, advertising successes such as the recent Macrosoft campaign, have raised the reliability and fame of our brand and the services we offer.

I feel proud to be able to make a commitment to you all, and, buoyed by the situation described above, I should like to personally inform you of my decision to offer my candidature for the position of manager and executive director to be voted on at the upcoming general meeting to be held in the first week of July.

I should also like to take this opportunity to congratulate and thank the individual who started our magnificent company, and who has occupied, until now, the post to which I aspire: Frank Wizard. His legacy is incredibly rich, but I believe that the time has come when we should move forward, to harvest more successes. We all want the best for our company.

During the two months which still remain before the general meeting I shall continue to work to win over those who are still not convinced they should give me their vote. I trust that their intelligence and the tangible results which have been achieved will break down barriers which are simply those of emotion.

I remain, as always, at your service.

W. West

The effect was paralysing. I had to read it through several times in order to make sure of two things. First, that she had managed to take over the success of our campaign, and secondly, that she really had decided to take over the leadership and unseat Frank. Her electoral campaign had begun, but what could I do to prevent the tyrannical finance manager from seizing the reins of the company?

I looked up from my computer and saw Lionel coming in through the door of my office. His face told me that he had already read the letter.

"You've read it? This is incredible. Who would have believed it?" he said indignantly.

"I know, Lionel, sit down, and calm down."

"We can't just sit on our hands! If Mrs. West is successful, bang goes our dream. The company will stifle imagination and start to prioritise profitability above everything else. I can see it coming, staff cutbacks, ludicrous budgets…"

"Look, of course you know she's not my favourite person, but hang on a minute. Where did the information come from? I think that a perception arising from her previous moves is one thing, but prophesying a definite future based on that is quite another. Am I right?"

"Are you trying to tell me that you don't think this is bad news?" he asked, mystified.

"No, Lionel, all I'm saying is that we mustn't plunge into hysteria or despair. She's getting ready to make a lunge to seize power and I guess she'll have a plan for the organisation, right? Okay, so before we start to decide what our situation really is, we need to be certain of all the facts. Let's go and talk to her."

"Go and talk to Mrs. West?"

"Of course. Anyway, she will need votes, and don't forget that as of July the first, I have a vote, too. Maybe she'll convince us."

"I doubt it, Dorothy. I just hope that you have some kind of plan in mind."

I don't know if my eyes showed what I was thinking, but what I was sure about was that the whole idea seemed so ghastly that my thinking was quite simple: in order not to become panic-stricken, we needed to know what her real intentions were.

A couple of minutes later, Oscar and Tim arrived in my office. I picked up the phone and rang the extension of the finance department.

"Mrs. West? This is Dorothy Grimm. I wonder if you could spare a little time to talk to some of the department managers just to clarify the information in the email we received this morning."

"Good morning, Dorothy. I shall be delighted to see you right away, if you'd like. I imagine you're referring to Timothy, Oscar and Lionel, as well as yourself, right?"

"That's right."

"Wonderful. I'll see you in my office within the hour, okay?"

"We'll see you then. Thanks."

"Looking forward to it," she said gaily.

I hung up and told my companions just what I'd been explaining a few moments before to Lionel. They were initially slightly unnerved, but then agreed and said that they could see that the best thing they could do was to make an opportunity to get started on the new project and find out just what was implied by such a controversial proposal.

Exactly thirty-eight minutes later Mrs. West's secretary told her boss that we were there, and asked us to step in.

The office was amazing, the walls papered in purple with greenish art nouveau details. The huge windows on the fortieth floor offered spectacular views of Manhattan. Mrs. West, impeccable as always, today in a mauve dress, was waiting for us.

"Please, take a seat. I'll deal with your uncertainties directly. But first of all, do you know Mr. Monk?" She introduced us to a man already seated on one of the couches with which the office was furnished.

I remembered Mr. Monk. He was the man who had been complaining to Miss Toto the first day I arrived at the office. His black suit and pale face gave evidence of no emotion whatsoever. When we turned to him he merely raised an eyebrow and turned back to the papers he was holding.

"Yes, I know Mr. Monk. He's the office security chief," Tim replied.

"That's right, and these people are Mrs. South, administrative manager, and Mr. Mombi, logistics head. They're here on the same mission as you."

"Pleased to meet you," I said.

"Well, since we're all here, we can begin." Mrs. West smiled.

"I'm sorry I'm late. Someone must have forgotten to tell me about this meeting."

It was Heidi North. She was as lovely as ever, with a radiant smile that seemed to complement her perfect white suit. She moved towards us, winked at me, and took a seat.

"Um, well, it was a rather unplanned meeting," Mrs. West explained rather uneasily.

"I find it slightly hard to believe that neither Frank nor any of the other members who will vote at the upcoming general meeting are here, but, well, I suppose on short notice…"

"Don't forget the investors' votes. They're worth twice the votes of those of us here, and their representative is also absent. I should say again that this is merely an informal meeting for information purposes, requested by some of our colleagues."

"I imagine you're feeling confident of the investors' votes and that's why they're not here. But let's cut to the chase. What, exactly, is your intention?"

"To run Oz Company in the best way possible, to transform this company into an empire the mere mention of which inspires respect, to make it a powerhouse creating successes of such importance that any business which thinks itself important will want us to handle its advertising."

"I must say I like the sound of that. We will develop a much stronger, more powerful image," remarked Mr. Monk.

"So how do you intend to achieve that?" asked Oscar.

"It's all been worked out. In the first place we have already begun to take over influential companies in a number of states. In the upcoming weeks they will begin to use our trade mark and pass their clients over to us. Negotiations have been successful on that front."

"A stable, consolidated company is such a pleasure to watch," put in Mrs. South.

"Furthermore, in the next few days our expansion will become effective in the twenty-two most powerful states in the USA. Representation like this has never been achieved before."

"How will it affect the personnel?" wondered Tim.

"As everybody knows, takeovers involve the optimisation of resources. We shall make use of the best people available to us, and the remainder will be relocated. If retrenchments are unavoidable they will, of course, take place in such a way that our overall budgets can be adjusted so as to be more efficient and effective."

"That's okay, there are certainly several people in my department who ought to be relocated," smiled Mr. Mombi.

"But there's plenty of time to make decisions on that score," said Mrs. West.

"Who will decide what the advertising campaigns are worth and defend them as far as the shareholders are concerned?" asked Lionel.

"As you know, that task always falls to the executive president. And since in recent times Frank has not been performing that function, it is my intention to personally supervise all projects so that they receive a balanced and even identity."

"What happens to Frank Wizard and Henry Baum?" I couldn't help asking.

Mrs. West's expression changed and she became nervous.

"Obviously, Frank will leave the command, although he will be appointed managing auditor. I'm afraid I'm not familiar with the other person."

She was lying, and the answers she had given my companions were in no way satisfactory. Having listened to Mrs. West's proposal and put up with her speech calling for votes we left and met with Heidi in her office on the forty-sixth floor.

"Unbelievable!" Lionel kept saying.

"So the situation is genuinely serious," Heidi interrupted him. "As far as we can tell Mrs. West's tactics are just a taste of what we can expect if she really seizes power. The cards are now on the table. On the one side are the votes of Monk, Mombi, South and West, on the other, our own. That would give us a win, but if we factor in the double value votes of the investors, our defeat is unavoidable."

"Is there anything we can do?" I wondered.

"There's just one option: put up a better candidate and fight it out with her."

"But who could we offer as a candidate?" said Oscar.

"Well that's obvious. It has to be Frank Wizard," I replied, while my companions sat in silence.

"I'm sorry to have to tell you, Dorothy... that won't be possible," Heidi gently said.

"Why not? I'm certain that when he finds out what's been happening he's bound to oppose it." My anxiety was apparent.

"For some years now Frank has been passing his work over to us, to me in particular. He lost interest in Oz when the investors forced him to change the company policy so that the tyranny of figures became paramount. He decided to lose himself in a little project that he's been working on all his life. It's now the only thing he cares about. He's not interested in Oz Company any more."

"Can't we convince him?"

"I'm afraid not, Dorothy, his road leads elsewhere and his decision is irreversible."

"But he has the casting vote," I explained. "If we can achieve a draw we can claim that vote, and that's the end of Mrs. West's candidature."

"I'm sorry, Dorothy, but as I've said, this is a really complicated situation."

"Well, I refuse to give in. If Frank won't stand, then I will!" My blood was up.

"Are you serious?" asked Tim.

"As you said yourself, we can't sit on our hands, so I've made my decision. I trust that you, too, all know what you have to do. So you'll have to excuse me – I have a great deal of work to do. I must examine the strengths and weaknesses of my opposing candidate."

Lionel smiled at Heidi and she returned the same conspiratorial smile to Oscar.

"Hold it right, there, Ginger – wrong again. It's not just you who have a lot of work to do – we *all* have a great deal of work to do. We're right behind you!"

12

The Guardian of the Gates

*"There is no such thing as a favourable wind
for he who doesn't know where he's going"*

Seneca

That particular morning I was in my office at the crack of
dawn, even before Boq, who was famous for being the first
to arrive for work. For a few moments I checked whether
you could see the offices in the buildings in front from
my own office. In one I could see a heated conversation
going on between a man who seemed to be the boss and
one of his colleagues. Several floors higher up a young man
was laughing at the antics of one of his companions. As I
watched I began to realise that for many people the office
is the most important part of their lives. They spend more
time there than in any other place, and the relationships
and situations they experience there inevitably affect their
behaviour in their private lives.

Only a few months before, when I arrived at this office,
I met dozens of people whom you could have called the
living dead, people who had once been alive, but who, little
by little, because of their lack of objectives and imagination,
had become souls in torment, wandering through their
offices without hope or life. They were people who were
on the run from talent, striving to beat down any semblance
of life in their environment. If a person who was really full
of life appeared, someone able to reveal to the dead what

they really were, the dead souls would simply try to drain off that vitality.

But I hadn't let that get me down. I see my business as bringing people back to life, and the job might be hard, but I can do it. Through communication and commitment, by getting colleagues more involved, giving them responsibility, offering tangible success, and making them take part in managerial decisions, some of the departments had regained an extraordinary level of life. Oscar, Tim and Lionel had adopted the same guidelines and were injecting vitality and excitement into their respective teams. We were all participants in the great campaign, we all energised the company. We brought the living dead back to real life.

But no-one can really leave the ranks of the living dead for good without an objective to reach, a goal, a dream. The success we had had would be a mere placebo if we failed to create an inspirational vision for each and every one of the staff at Oz Company. Mrs. West had created and developed her own, and although I might not like it one little bit, it had to be admitted that she had done her duty. At that moment I remembered a device which Henry showed me to work out what the next step should be in moments of doubt.

I sat down at my desk, took out a sheet of clean paper, and drew a series of circles linked horizontally like a chain, and at either side two larger rings. In the circle at the left I wrote today, and in the last one, winning the votes of the board of directors. The idea was to fill in the circles one by one, from the one furthest from today to the one nearest to my first space always responding to the same prompt: if I want… for that I need…

This way I started filling in the following circle by completing the sentence: if I want to win the votes of the board of directors, for that I need to convince the rest of the meeting that my proposal is better. In this way I continued to answer the questions and filling in the circles until I reached one in which I wrote, create a more brilliant alternative without giving up on economic efficiency.

Thus I realised that in order to beat Mrs. West I had to take part in the game and compete using the same weapons as her. I had to create a vision which would respect the values which Frank Wizard outlined for this company, but which could also be adapted to meet the new intentions of the investors.

I took out another sheet and in large letters I wrote the following: greatness lies in simple ideas, niches in the market, be the joker in the pack, an albino tiger in a zoo of colours, be different, unique and small, universal ideas = international clients.

I began to smile as I took stock of the situation. I had at last located my tigon, and this was the circus which was waiting for me. Now all I had to do was tame it.

Oscar then appeared in my office, together with Tim and Lionel, looking very pleased with themselves. They were in a very good mood and seemed particularly happy. I had to ask.

"What's happening?"

"Hurry come with us, Frank is in the building."

"What?" I was amazed.

"Miss Toto just called me. Frank Wizard was seen going up to his office first thing in the morning. We have to have a meeting with him to tell him what's going on. Now's your chance. Let's go!"

They didn't have to say another word. I jumped up and grabbed my cell phone and ideas notebook, and scurried off with my colleagues.

"We're off to see Mr. Wizard!" I sang out in excitement.

"The wonderful owner of Oz!" Lionel finished for me.

As we went down in the elevator we couldn't help exchanging excited looks. There was no question about it, Mr. Wizard was the only person who could help us and we just had to see him. After so much doubt and uncertainty, at last we had him in the building.

When we reached the entrance hall Miss Toto caught sight of us and came running towards us.

"Take it easy, now, take it easy, everything's okay," she calmed us down.

As she took her place beside us, clutching all Mr. Wizard's back mail, she cried excitedly:

"We're off to see Mr. Wizard!"

"The wonderful owner of Oz" laughed Tim and Oscar.

We burst out into another round of laughter which seemed to give us strength as we made for the yellow and gold elevator.

As we approached it we saw the bad-tempered man with the funny moustache looking us up and down.

"Where do you think you're going?" he snapped.

"We're just taking the elevator, if it's any of your business," I smiled back.

"This is the yellow elevator, nobody takes the yellow elevator. The yellow elevator goes straight to the rooms occupied by Mr. Frank Wizard, the owner of this company," he replied with his usual coolness and air of respect.

"We are aware of that," said Miss Toto. "That's why we're taking the elevator. I have to take this urgent information up, and these people, members of the board of directors, need to see the President."

"I'm sorry, but Mr. Wizard is seeing no-one today, for any reason whatsoever."

"But it's urgent!" I returned.

"For any reason whatsoever!" he snapped irritably.

"But this is Dorothy, and she must see Mr. Wizard," said Oscar.

"Dorothy? The girl who confronted Mrs. West?" His tone suddenly changed. "Okay, wait here, I'll tell Mr. Wizard that you need to see him."

Excitement returned to our faces when we heard these words. At last we would be able to seek Frank's help at this crucial moment.

The guardian of the elevator turned away from us for a moment to speak on the intercom, and then said:

"Mr. Wizard will meet you on floor fifty-seven, in the meeting room."

The doors of the wonderful elevator opened and we walked in, thanking the man with the moustache for his kindness. Inside we noticed that the floor was made up of small yellow tiles, all perfectly fitted. The metal frame, a small handrail and the control panel, were also gilded. There were only two buttons on the control panel with two numbers; fifty-seven and fifty-eight. The first operated by itself and the doors of the elevator slowly closed. The glass walls and ceiling provided us with a fantastic view when, once we had risen above the twenty-fifth floor, we were clear of the rest of the buildings and were surrounded by the incredible panorama.

We were looking out at New York in action, the office lights still on where people had worked through the night, a horizon of great avenues, huge wall of glass and mirrors. Everything, including the most modern roofs, was beneath our feet, and before our eyes there appeared the fantastic image of the sun, telling us that we were in for another wonderful spring day. For just a few moments there was silence, and our thoughts were occupied with pleasant matters.

"Floor fifty-seven. Have a nice day," said the automatic voice.

We all turned and smiled at each other, and the doors opened to reveal a huge room which took up half the floor of the building. A spacious entrance hall opened onto more than a hundred seats facing a table set up on a stage. Around the table a number of chairs were arranged with names on them: Mombi, South, Monk and West on one side, Frank in the centre, and Heidi, Lionel, Tim, Oscar and Dorothy on the other. That was the first time I had seen my chair, and I realised how important a person I was in the company.

On the stage a huge screen showed an image of the Oz Company logo. As we were walking along the central aisle of the room towards the stage a somewhat distorted voice caused us to stop.

"Good morning, colleagues."

"G-Good morning, Mr. Wizard," I said, rather nervously.

"Excuse the fact that I am unable to join you. My schedule today is very tight, and I was not expecting your visit. But tell me, how can I help you?"

I started to explain what had been going on in the company recently, how Mrs. West was controlling the company, using the budgets as a means of stifling the departments. As I was explaining my companions' situation, Frank interrupted.

"A research manager who believed he had lost his brain, a production manager without a heart and a communication chief who is too cowardly to face the situation. Obviously I didn't expect that of you when you became part of the Oz family. And yet, fortunately, it seems that something has changed in the past few weeks, wouldn't you say?"

"One thing I can be sure of is that on the positive front it is Dorothy's arrival which has turned things around. She has been a gale of fresh air, and it has really just revived us – it's been a revolution for us all," said Miss Toto.

"She showed me that if I had vision, a clear mind and the abil-ity to make the most of my resources, then my brain was working perfectly," said Oscar, resting his eyes on me as a sign of support.

"I have to admit that I had forgotten my heart. But she showed me how to create emotions, to empathise and fill hearts with feeling," said Tim. "Now I am so much stronger."

"And I faced up to my fears, set uncertainty aside, and managed to find the courage to defend my ideas against detractors," Lionel concluded.

"Well, it looks as though we did the right thing when we hired this young lady. Well done, Dorothy." Frank's slow voice was heard. "But if everything is well, I don't understand why you need my help."

"A more serious threat is hanging over our heads. Mrs. West wants to take control of the company and discard the values which you yourself set up for this company," I put in anxiously.

"Those values vanished from these walls long ago."

"Well, I haven't given them up," I said hotly. "I believe in a tolerant, friendly, respectable and respectful business, one which creates brilliant and simple ideas, but which are powerful. I believe in a clean business. That is what attracted me to Oz and I'm not about to turn my back on that. I have decided to fight to retain your legacy and I will confront the tyranny of the figures which Mrs. West intends to impose."

Frank was silent for a long moment. Then the distorted voice said:

"My dear friends, let's do something. As you know, I have been somewhat uninvolved with this project of late, but if you can get together a better project and in that way unseat Mrs. West, I will certainly give you my vote. On that you can rely. Now, I must apologise, but I shall have to leave you, as I have, as I said, a very tight schedule today. I trust you and your abilities."

After these words the screen switched off and with it disappeared the poor communication which had governed the conversation.

We took the down elevator somewhat depressed to realise that Frank had by no means given us the commitment we had wished for. As soon as we were all in the elevator, the doors began to slowly close.

"So what was all that about?" Miss Toto wondered incredulously.

"I was really hoping for a better response than that," said Tim.

"Yes. After all, it's his business we're trying to save," added Oscar.

"Do you really see it like that?" I asked sceptically.

"Well, he hasn't got very involved, has he?" replied Lionel.

"So how do you see the situation?" I asked him.

"Well, I see something very different. I've seen someone who wants you to fight for your dream and wants you to fight hard. He wants you to construct a unique project. He has confidence in you, but if he had said that whatever you did he would support you, he would be false to his own way of thinking. He wants brilliant and inspirational people. Frank always wanted the best people around him, and this is your chance to show him that that's what you are."

"Yes, but we have so little time to come up with a project on that scale, bearing in mind the fact that Mrs. West has had months to prepare the ground."

"Just listen to me for one moment, because I'm only going to tell you once," said Miss Toto.

> "Pietro Molieri was without a doubt the best pastry cook in the whole of Rome. His amazing chocolate and strawberry cake was so good that every morning there would be people swarming in front of his counter for the first cakes of the day to come out of the oven so that they could have one for breakfast. There were even people who came from nearby cities to buy his cakes on a weekly basis.
>
> "People said that it was a genuine explosion of flavour. It was a soft, sponge-type cake containing beads of chocolate which slowly melted in the mouth creating a

total sensation that was impossible to describe. The final effect was a crunchy biscuit base which rounded off this delicious mouthful with a taste that was worthy of the best kitchens in Europe.

"Pietro was an institution, and people used to congratulate him when around midday, when his day's work ended, he took a stroll in the Coliseum area and had a coffee at the trattoria owned by his friend Fabio Bellagio.

"But not everybody was pleased with his success. Leonardo Medici, his young and impulsive assistant, couldn't stand the fact that no-one recognised his skill or his part in the work. The way he saw things, it was he who did almost all the work, so he deserved the same praise as his boss.

"So one day Leonardo decided to steal the recipe and make his own strawberry and chocolate cakes in a nearby bakery. Very sure of himself, and with the guarantee of having done the work thousands of times, he made a big show of advertising his upcoming opening. And as if that were not enough, he decided to lower the price, to make sure that the customers would have no reason for staying away.

"On the day he was to open his business, Leonardo took out the recipe and checked to make sure that he had all the ingredients. The best Spanish flour, the creamiest Greek yoghurt, the thickest Belgian chocolate and perfect French strawberries. Fresh eggs, biscuits baked the day before by himself and the sweetest sugar from the south of Italy completed the list.

"Step by step, he scrupulously followed all the instructions set down on the recipe. He made absolutely sure of the quantities, the times and even the temperature of the oven. And at last, while the first cakes were still in the oven, the customers were already waiting in front of the counter of the new cake shop.

"When Leonardo cut out the first portions, the wonderful smell spread out through the neighbourhood. When a customer took the first portion and popped it into his mouth, he immediately sensed the sponginess of the cake, and everybody could see how the chocolate slowly melted. But something was wrong. The cake didn't taste the same. Nobody could say exactly what was missing, but it was simply not the same.

"Irritated, Leonardo closed the shop and on the following morning he went through the steps one by one, doing it even more carefully this time, if that were possible. But when the first customers showed up, the response did not vary: it's not the same. He continued to try for a few more days, but always got the same outcome. The cake was very, very good, but it was not like Pietro's cake.

"At last, in desperation, yielding to the inevitable, he shut down the shop and after waiting until all the customers had finished up all the delicacies in Pietro Molieri's shop, he went in, begged forgiveness, and asked if he could have his old job back. The famous pastry cook gave him an understanding look and said: 'Leonardo, you've been working for me for years. It really is time you spread your wings and flew.' The young man, confused, replied: 'But Maestro, I'll never be like you. Everybody has told me that my cakes just aren't the same as yours.' Pietro thought for a moment, and then answered: 'Nor will they ever be. You know absolutely everything which is written down in a recipe. You have done the work with a technical skill which I never had. And yet, our products are different. But I know the people and I know that their lives are awkward and difficult. So every morning, while they eat my cakes, they enjoy a few moments of absolute happiness. That's where the difference lies.' Young Leonardo, still not understanding, asked him to explain a little more, and the great maestro Pietro, before he said farewell to his companion of many years, replied: 'I prepare the cakes with the aim that my customers will have a moment of intense pleasure while they eat their slices, and I'm thinking about their smiles and I'm thinking about making them happy. You, on the other hand, were only thinking about beating me.' "

dos tartas y un café

dos para llevar

un capuccino!

13

Monk Attacks

*"Only mediocre people are
always at their best"*

Somerset Maugham

Dear colleagues,

*My name is Dorothy Grimm and for several months now
I have been the manager of the creative department of Oz
Company.*

*To work in this company would be a dream for anybody in-
volved in the world of advertising - a sound company, with
almost unlimited funds and the very highest profile. Surrounded by brilliant colleagues, with talented management,
we have built a company based on the values of tolerance,
respect, creativity, innovation and the very best treatment
for our campaigns and, naturally, for our staff.*

*When I walked through the door for the first time, I read
that famous sentence "Greatness lies in simple ideas", but
after a few months working at Oz, I realised that the only
aspect of that dream which I talked to you about before was
that sentence in emerald letters over the door.*

*We all know that we have to be more profitable to continue
to be competitive. Nobody denies the fact that a larger war
chest is a real life-raft in a turbulent world such as ours.*

However, as I and my team showed during the last campaign, not only are both ideas perfectly compatible, they actually must be complementary if we wish to continue to be the company we once were.

Thanks to the negotiations undertaken by the finance department, in the upcoming weeks we shall be graced with branches in the most powerful states in the country. But they will never become true representatives of Oz if they fail to learn the philosophy which made this company great. If we fail to recover the importance of ideas and the power of the talent within the company, these new offices and the headquarters, they will lose the identity which once so inspired you.

Remember the last time you smiled when you got up in the morning and got ready for work charged with stimulating energy. This is the inspiration I beg you to recover. And I shall work to achieve that. But obviously, I shall need your help.

It's time we re-discovered our motivation, began to feel once again part of a great shared project. It's time for us to take control of our new life, to decide what we want and what we don't want. Let's move away from these dark times in which we have all felt lost and isolated. Let's re-discover the strength which made us great and show the world that there is another way to run a business.

In just a few weeks I shall be offering myself as a candidate for the position of president of Oz and I am using this letter to tell you about my intentions and the all-inclusive nature of my project. I know where I want to go, where I want to take the company. Which means that only one question remains – are you coming with me?

Dorothy Grimm

This was how I summed up my intentions in a letter which I sent out to each and every one of the company staff members, whether they held a vote or not. The idea was to imbue all the staff with the spirit and need for change. It's important for people to understand that they can count on you and that the importance of their support for your project is crucial for it to work. The response was quick in coming.

My own colleagues who, with the exception of Boq, were not expecting this decision, once they had checked their email and read the letter, jumped to their feet and with huge pleasure came over to congratulate me on my decision and tell me they were ready to take on the project. It was fantastic to realise that in me they recognised the skills needed to lead the change.

Other messages of support and encouragement soon appeared, and when I visited another department or the cafeteria, there was no shortage of colleagues who stopped to wish me luck. A new feeling had appeared in the company. People needed to believe in a new direction, one which would replace the sad, fearful and dark road they had been obliged to follow.

Naturally Mrs. West rapidly sent her reply and in a brief email wished me luck. Maybe she didn't take me seriously or perhaps she thought I had no chance. Even so, she forwarded to me the specifications for a fresh campaign: promoting the Mugatu Design season.

According to the client, this company's shoes had turned into something very select, and they thought they were becoming too elitist. They weren't overly concerned about this, but they were worried that their brand was becoming detached from their company image. They wanted to transform the firm into an object of desire, a dream that was achievable. We needed to project the image that with a pair of Mugatu shoes you could achieve your goals, so that everybody would want to own a pair.

There was no more information, no patterns or models they wanted to promote... nothing. It was just a campaign to sell the brand and the general concept that their shoes were a talisman for success. They certainly had been in my case.

I got the team together and explained the details of the new campaign to them. We would have to execute it to perfection, riding on the new, dominant feeling.

Before the meeting ended, Tim and Lionel came into the department and sat down in some of the chairs to wait. Oscar appeared a few minutes later. When the meeting at last came to an end we had a further meeting in the glass room so that nothing we said would be misunderstood by my colleagues.

"Everything is going great, Ginger! All my people are really excited about our decision and are beginning to spread the good news to colleagues and friends in other department!" said Tim.

"We've managed to send a clear message, with no small print, stating the desired objective and placing it within the reach of all. I think this is a really exciting speech," Lionel concluded.

"Well, I have fresh news for you, gentlemen. We have to create a new campaign for Mugatu Design. I received the specifications from Mrs. West this very day."

"She is so shifty! She wants us to be too tied up with this project to be able to devote any energy to our own," commented the offended Oscar.

"Do you think that's her plan?"

"Look," I replied, taking up the jug of water that was on the table, "this is our strength in the candidature. We're all in this jug, concentrating our attention and our power. But if I do something natural," I said, pouring water from the jug into the glasses, "I manage to ensure that your glasses are full of other tasks and the overall project loses a considerable mount of its strength."

"Very smart!" said Tim.

"Anyway, we're not out to name the guilty, we're out to turn situations to our advantage. We must re-use their strength for our own benefit," I told them calmly.

"But how? We shall be really busy with the new campaign, so we shall hardly be in a position to run a project aimed at convincing the investors and the rest of the board."

"Actually, she doesn't realise what a favour she's done us," I said, taking my glass and putting it inside the jug.

"I think I get it. We have to put the two ideas together, right?" said Tim, taking his glass and Lionel's and putting them both inside the jug.

"Precisely! We shall transform the Mugatu project into our own campaign," concluded Oscar as, since his glass was also now inside the jug, the increase in mass caused the water to spill over onto the table.

"This is our strength. All she's done is supply us with another device whereby our talent can overflow," said Lionel.

"That's all very well, but now we have to find a cloth to clear this mess up!" I smiled at my laughing companions.

In the next few hours, in a meeting with an assortment of our colleagues from all departments, we began to study the options, my colleagues' ideas and the various proposals that had been offered. We analysed the way they would be produced and subsequently communicated. If we felt like it, we moved on to another selection, and if there was something that didn't work, we discarded it in favour of a better study.

Uncle Henry came into my mind, since it would have been the day before that he would have met with W. West. I felt distracted by this thought, and wondered what had been happening down on the Farm, so I excused myself, rose from the meeting table, and went to give him a call. The phone rang a few times, and then...

"Freckles, good morning!"

"Hi, Uncle Henry. I have been so wanting to talk to you!"

"Before you say anything else, let me congratulate you in person for the butterflies campaign. It was sensational. Worthy of record as a real advertising legend."

"Is that the opinion of Henry Baum?" I smiled over the wire.

"It sure is! Ha, ha, ha."

"So tell me, to what do I owe the pleasure of this call, young lady?"

"It's like this – I'm really worried about your situation and that of your company. As you know, Oz Company is in the process of taking over a number of companies throughout the country and I have to know whether your meetings are taking that kind of direction."

Henry was quiet for a while. At last he gave me the bad news.

"These are different times, Dorothy. Us old guys just can't fight against young people hungry for power. I wish I could tell you something else, but I can't. I'm sorry."

"What are you trying to tell me, Henry?"

"It seems they've had it all worked out for over a year. They've put me in an impossible situation. If I don't agree to the merger, they're going to open some huge offices just a few streets away from us, in a larger building and with a much more powerful image."

"The clients will stay loyal to you!" I tried to encourage him.

"Don't be naive, Freckles. The clients will stay with me for dinner and will keep on sending a Christmas gift, but they'll give their advertising campaigns to whoever can give them the best quality under the best financial conditions. Anyhow, a superpower like Oz won't waste any time coming up with a salary policy to head-hunt my most talented people."

"You can't let it happen!" I cried indignantly.

"Nor would I, Freckles, but these people have won the battle even before we get our war paint on."

"Oh, Henry, I'm so sorry. So what happens now?"

"Take it easy, Dorothy, something tells me I shall still be Henry for quite some time yet. I'll get the company ready for the merger, I'll try to make sure that they respect my employees' working conditions and I'll start having meetings with the clients. I must try to ensure that the procedure takes place without any personal or professional losses on the part of our people. And when it's over, I'll have a drink with you on some wonderful beach and we'll just laugh at the whole situation. I shall never desert the Farm I can assure you of that, even if they name it Oz Company Kansas."

It was simply incredible, but there was no doubt that the tone of Henry's voice was much sadder than usual, so I tried to encourage him, removing the sting from the situation, telling him that he'd be able to adapt. Mostly I was just amazed at his generosity. He was willing to give up his dream as long as his staff retained their employment conditions.

A few more minutes chatting with him about my situation in the company, the new decisions they had taken and my plan to become the new President of Oz seemed to give me strength. Even if there had been small reason for my decision, there was now a very good one. I would not let the spirit of the Farm disappear. If it lay in my power, I would do exactly the opposite: I would draw that spirit into this multinational.

When I hung up, my colleagues softly asked me what was happening. As I explained the situation, they showed their anger. Little by little I managed to transform their fury into strength to achieve our objective. It was important for us not to waste our energies and to remain focussed. Henry had taught me that years ago, and now I was going to put it into practice.

"Miss Dorothy Grimm?" asked a young man wearing the uniform of the security corps.

"That's me."

"This letter is for you. It's from Mr. Monk."

Dear colleagues,

In the past few days an accusation based on solid facts has placed the security service of this company on the alert.

It would appear that one or more employees of this company are taking our ideas and using our work procedures for the benefit of our competitors.

For this reason all heads of department are hereby informed that as of now a security officer will be present in each section to protect our interests.

I would be grateful if you would accept this officer as just another colleague and allow him to be a part of your teams. I shall send further information as soon as possible. I hope that we shall soon be able to adopt an appropriate action and everything will be back to normal.

Thank you for your co-operation. I remain completely at your service.

Yours sincerely,
F. Monk
Head of Security

"I'm glad I find you here with Mr. Crow, Mr. Mann and Mr. Kövard. Here are their letters," said the young man, handing over the envelopes.

"What can this mean?" wondered Lionel.

"This is just a show of power on the part of Mrs. West. She's very smart, and she knows that the only way she can maintain the illusion of dominance is by demonstrating that her eyes are everywhere. I can just imagine her with Mr. Monk, telling him: 'I want your boys to bring me all the information they can as fast as possible. Go, fly!' "

"How does this affect us?" asked Tim.

"Well, if we can re-route this new attack, it will make us even stronger. We will have to communicate to our colleagues how important it is to create a new way to run the company. Oscar, you must get to work on the new campaign, we must come up with something that not only convinces the client but also tips the balance of the shareholders' votes in our favour. Tim, you must reach the hearts and minds of the staff and get them to believe in a new goal. Then we'll have a meeting with you to analyse production for the Mugatu campaign. While you, Lionel, must gather all your courage and confront Mrs. West face to face. Tell her our intentions, that not a single staff member or investor will be unaware of our project."

Off they scurried to their stations, now shadowed by Mr. Monk's people. We had a new job to do, and we had to be perfectly co-ordinated to execute it.

Then I had an idea. It was simple, effective and powerful enough to come out on top. I had a meeting with Boq to tell him about it, asked him to be very discrete, but to make sure that it was slowly communicated to all the members of the department, without the security spies finding out.

"Is that possible?" he asked me.

"Only Oscar has the answer. We have to rely on him."

I called Oscar to put him in the picture. It was a serious challenge, but I was sure that a person with his brain and such a skilled team would manage to make it work. I asked him to pass the message on to the colleagues and to be very ready with his leaks. This was the ace up our sleeve, and we couldn't afford to fail.

I left the office, hailed a cab and went home. I climbed the three floors by the stairs, opened the huge wooden door and made straight for the Mugatu shoe box.

As I made my way towards Central Park with my shoes under my arm, I paused at a site where some work was going on and asked them for a little cement powder. They gave me some in a bag, and thanking them I took it in my other hand. I had all the ingredients I needed.

On reaching Central Park, I sought out the sand where the children played. I poured a little water from my bottle, and sprinkled the cement in a little space about thirty centimetres square. I took out my right shoe, put it on, and stamped firmly on the cement powder. The imprint was perfect, with the beautiful M on the sole, the symbol of the Mugatu Design logo, perfectly readable. I took a number of black and white photos with my mobile phone, and when I had more than ten which were very good I hurried to wash the shoes at a nearby fountain. I really would have hated to damage my shoes because of a little cement.

Reach for the Stars!

14

Dorothy's Magic Arts

"The first time you deceive me, you are to blame; the second time, I am"

Arab proverb

A few days later the famous photo of the footprint had been sufficiently leaked and practically the whole of the staff were talking about the campaign: a simple black and white photograph of a mark on cement. It was an ingenious and cheap way of showing that, with a pair of Mugatus, everybody could make it and leave their footprints at the Chinese theatre in Hollywood Boulevard. The provisional slogan, "Reach for the Stars" did the rest.

The production team started to produce black and white photocopies of the footprint with the slogan already made up, to be precise a million of them. The cost of this leaflet was barely seventy-three thousand dollars. Copies were stored in a warehouse owned by the company, waiting for the order to be given for them to be spread out all over the city.

That morning I happened to meet Mrs. West in the elevator. She was dressed in a marvellous pistachio coloured jacket with chocolate seams. Her handbag and shoes were the same shade of brown. She cut a real dash.

"Good morning, Ginger," she greeted me as though it was funny.

"Good morning, Mrs. West."

"Congratulations on the Mugatu campaign. It's rather less surprising than I expected, but you've certainly kept the cost down to an amazing level."

"We've tried to respect the client's requirements and the new company philosophy. After all, the investors want profitability, right?"

"Of course. Even so, I'm not sure that the client will be one hundred per cent satisfied with a footprint in cement in Hollywood Boulevard. It's hardly what you would call out of the ordinary," she was saying as we reached floor twelve. "This is your stop, Dorothy, I have further up to go."

"This is my floor at the moment," I replied firmly. "But don't worry, the campaign will meet with more approval than you imagine."

"I've got quite a lot of imagination, Ginger," she declared as the doors closed.

The bait had been cast, and the fish had taken the hook. And the results started to appear that very morning. Roger, the security officer who had been imposed on us only a week before told me that his new orders were to resume normal duties. The spies were being withdrawn.

"As easy as that?" a curious Boq wondered.

"Yes, Boq. Mrs. West knew that this campaign was crucial for our bid for the presidency. If we did something really spectacular she would have found out all the secrets, so that she would have been able to countermand them with her own actions."

"But this campaign is spectacular," said the confused Boq.

"She doesn't think so. This is just a sensationalist campaign affecting everybody who thinks they can become a Hollywood star. It's something which is hardly original and which she thinks the investors will see as a drag on our bid."

"But that isn't really the case." Boq smiled.

"She'll base her attack on convincing the investors that the "Butterflies" campaign was a flash in the pan. Certainly an indication of talent, but immature and lacking permanence when it comes to taking over a major project."

"I sure hope you're right and it comes out okay."

"I'm sure of it. Now we must press on. Would you call a meeting with Oscar and Tim, in Lionel's office in an hour. We must get ready for the big general meeting."

I took time out to send a message to all the staff telling them to send me their requests or wishes, the things they wanted changed or improved within the company, and saying that I would attach my management programme. All requests would be dealt with, and when the board had studied them, approval would be given to those that really improved the quality and well-being needed for the staff to perform their duties within the company.

It was crucial for the requests to be dealt with. You can never help anyone unless you've listened to them carefully. If we wanted to make a bid for a new business model, we had to start with the employees' needs.

Just forty-six minutes after sending the email, I was arriving in Lionel's office. My companions were already there.

"Congratulations, Dorothy," said Oscar, "that really does show brains."

"Thanks, but we still have to launch the campaign. Everything has to come out well. We have a great deal riding on this."

"Don't worry. This campaign will touch the hearts of millions."

"That's what I'm banking on, Tim," I answered.

"And what's more, it's a very brave move. You're one hell of an example to follow."

"Coming from you, Lionel, that's praise indeed. Have we fixed the day?"

"It's going to be Friday, June the twenty-eighth, so we have a week. It will be a lovely summer night. The sky will be completely clear and it will be very mild. On top of that, Mrs. West has already given her imprimatur. Her exact words were: 'I'm glad you've chosen a day with such good weather, I shall be enjoying a glass of Möet on the terrace at Shabay to celebrate having won the presidency.' "

"Great. Now we have to get ready for the campaign launch."

I started out by explaining that it was crucial that the campaign should be distributed in the days preceding the meeting, to strike a blow in our support for the meeting on the twenty-eighth.

"What I don't understand is where you got the idea from," mused Oscar.

"I remembered a quotation from Machiavelli: 'Everybody sees what you appear to be, few feel what you are.' "

As I spoke the line, I understood that we move according to perceptions and projection. Even though we may not want to, we allow ourselves to be led by our first impressions and we seldom change our minds. The fact is that we are usually surprised when someone shows us something which we had not initially perceived.

We usually act without realising that everything is recorded in the minds of those around us. If we act in a gentle and affectionate way, we form an opinion of ourselves which fulfils those requirements. If we are unpunctual or work in an excessively conscientious way we also reflect that. All of our projects form our personal brand.

Bearing this in mind, I realised that if we use projections well, people will see what we are keen to boost. And if we can do that with our own character or personality, how much easier would it be with this project!

"Is it really that easy?"

"Nobody said it was going to be easy, Tim. First you must know yourself, be aware of your strengths and weaknesses, then choose what you want to project and on that basis, be very consistent about imprinting this brand on everything you do."

"I get the picture, Dorothy, but I wasn't talking about one's personal brand. I was concerned with deceiving Mrs. West."

"In theory this follows the premise laid down by the great Houdini: 'You can't make a lion disappear. All you can do is distract attention sufficiently for others to get it off the stage.'"

"Ha, ha, distracting attention – how do we do that?" laughed Lionel.

"We have now revealed what we want and Mrs. West has seen what we wanted her to see. That makes it easy for us to strike a blow she is not expecting. How is your job proceeding, Oscar?"

"My team and I have been working on it for some weeks, and in a couple of days we should be ready to start testing. We're keeping our fingers crossed."

"I'd prefer to have it all cut and dried, rather than trusting to luck," commented Tim.

"What if the plan doesn't work?"

"If it really doesn't work we'll be in quite an awkward position. It will certainly affect our candidature and the inspiration of the staff. But remember, plan B is already under way. The "Reach for the Stars" campaign stands as a campaign supporting image and brand, and although it leaves us open to the criticisms of Mrs. West, we should be ready to defend it as strongly as possible."

"Anyhow, I feel confident that everything will turn out for the best," said Oscar. "You can put your faith in my brain."

"We all do, be sure of it. I think I speak for everybody when I say that you can rely on us if you need to," said Lionel.

"I know. Still, today's Friday. Relax this weekend and regain your strength. From Monday onwards we have a great deal of work to do and that's when I'll need you. My team and I will be working very hard over these days and on Sunday I'll start testing. I hope to be able to give you good news."

We said goodbye and wished each other a good weekend. As I'm sure my companions did also, I returned to the department to tidy up the last odds and ends of work and wish everybody a nice weekend. The cards were on the table, and I was sure that this game would be the toughest battle I had had to fight in a long time.

Paying heed to what Oscar had said, I decided to set aside some quality time for myself that weekend.

Saturday morning I slipped on something comfortable, and once I'd called my family and friends to keep them up to date with how things were, I set out for a stroll along Sixth Avenue. After a lengthy walk I stopped for a cappuccino and blueberry cheesecake at the café on the corner of Sixth and Broadway. That moment was always special, seated behind the glass watching people walking up and down the great avenue. Hundreds of tourists were there, their busy cameras ceaselessly snapping everything that moved. It amused me to think that maybe that couple would decide to put the snap that was immortalising this moment in this place in their living room. And if they were to look at the window behind the couple they would have seen me enjoying my coffee, peaceful and happy for ever. I finished my snack and walked on.

Six blocks further on, just a step from Times Square, between fortieth and forty-second street, I discovered what would come to be my favourite corner of the city: Bryant Park.

It was located next to a public library, which was always satisfying when you came to get information about a new campaign, and it was the largest park in Midtown Manhattan. I think what I liked most about this place what that, once I found out about its history, it gave forth a strong spirit of versatility and adaptation to change.

It appeared that it had been a cemetery for twenty years until urban expansion made it part of the city. Only ten years after it was closed it became the venue for the first Universal Exhibition in New York in the mid-nineteenth century. A crystal palace was built for the occasion which burnt down six years later.

At the end of the nineteenth century the park was in need of reconstruction, but that didn't happen until after the Great Depression, when the Parks Commissioner, Robert Moses, decided to rebuild it according to a design by Lusby Simpson. Despite the fact that it was intended to a peaceful place of rest and relaxation, it degenerated until it was only frequented by delinquents and beggars over the nineteen-seventies. Once again Bryant Park was in need of a facelift which took place over the nineteen eighties, to be re-opened to the public in 1992.

It was now, once again, a green and pleasant place, perfect for resting, strolling and reading. It also boasted a WiFi network, which meant that it was a good place to stay connected to the office and maybe do some work. But that weekend I was doing no work.

After my stroll and rest in the park, I decided to take myself to Juvenex Spa for a relaxing massage to relieve the tension which had accumulated. That wonderful sensation of the stones on my back undoubtedly calmed and reinvigorated me.

A lamb's lettuce salad, a salmon *sashimi* amazingly carved like a rose and fish in the Bann, left me entirely satisfied.

To end my day I decided on a peaceful walk home. I was surprised to realise how many hours had passed doing little more than stare at shop windows, buildings and advertising posters.

When at last I reached home I went for a comforting shower, thinking what a great day it had been. I realised how important it had been for body and mind to be able to rest. I felt fresh, cosseted and satisfied. We all need to set aside some time for ourselves from time to time to forget the troubles of the working week.

They say that the Vikings loved resting. They felt that it was important for warriors to rest, and punished those who disturbed the rest of the most courageous members of the community. They knew and understood that everyone needs to rest the body so that their work may be more efficient, but what is surprising is that they supported psychological or mental relaxation. They avoided stressing their sailors or burdening them with too much information so that they would have a much clearer view of the purpose of their campaign. They knew that a relaxed, fresh mind would think more effectively, would be much more ready to see understand better and would arrive at more reliable solutions to the problems they would encounter.

At that moment I felt very much like a Viking, in my own way, of course. I knew that the battle was already starting and that everything was ready. I was fully aware what my weapons were, and even had a good idea where the enemy would attack from. At least, so I thought, although as it turned out the following days had one or two surprises in store for me which would cause me to radically change my original position.

I don't know whether it was the image of the battle, or because the helmet and armour were so heavy, but barely second after I had finished drying my hair I fell exhausted into the arms of Morpheus.

15

Confronting W. West

"In order to teach all men to speak the truth, it is essential for them to learn to hear it"

Samuel Johnson

On Monday morning I felt that my walk to work was much more invigorating than usual. I felt like a new woman, and my mind was full of energy and motivation.

Over the weekend I had been able not only to fine tune my objective, but I had also managed to analyse and assess possible scenarios regarding the general meeting on the following Friday.

I began the week in a decisive mood, and it was clear that I must provide the staff with the outline of a project which harked back to the company's original values, albeit focusing firmly on a fresh future in which all could participate and believe.

I must also be able to convince the members of the board that I was in possession of all that was required to run and manage the company correctly. The more technical managers would have to see me as a demanding, decided and stable person, and, of course one who was resolute and efficient. Managers on the other side would have to see me as credible and reliable, and that my most highly developed abilities were inspiration, empathy and tenacity.

But there was a third side to the triangle: the investors. They needed to see in me a person capable of growing the company, of raising the business to heights which it had never before attained, and also of earning for them a very great deal of money. All this had to be done in five days, without lying to, or deceiving, anybody.

This was quite a fearsome challenge, particularly given that there were now many people who had placed their trust in me. I was determined to do absolutely everything in my power to ensure that Oz Company once again became that factory of dreams and inspiration that it had been.

To my surprise, Oscar, Tim and Lionel were waiting for me at the entrance door of the office that morning. All had a smile on their lips and an air of ease about them.

"Good morning, Ginger. Are you ready to begin?"

"We couldn't let you go in all by yourself on the first day of the big week." Tim shook his head.

"Thanks for that, but you really needn't have bothered."

"Of course we didn't," said Lionel, "we just really wanted to."

"Okay, okay, let's not start getting emotional, there's a great deal to be done," Oscar concluded.

As I passed through the doors of the office there was Miss Toto at her information desk, tipping me a wink. All the rest of the security and reception staff who were to be found there were watching us with looks of encouragement and approval. The positive spirit of our project was spreading. The minutes which followed as we rose to floor twelve needed to be savoured.

I moved to my desk and began to co-ordinate the actions we were going to carry out. The most important were to be at meetings with the Mugatu representatives to explain the campaign to them and to start, assuming they were in agreement, to distribute the copies we had made of the photograph of the footprint. I told Boq to begin to get the distribution and poster gluing teams ready. If all went well, we would be launching the campaign that night.

However, not that I was not expecting it, Mrs. West also had a card up her sleeve. Sometime towards midday on that Monday, a few minutes before it became official, Lionel Kövard called me to let me know that a press conference was going to be held to state that Oz Company was at last merging with the fifteen companies which were most representative of their respective states. This second takeover would make our company the most powerful in the country and one of the largest in the world.

I rapidly read through the internal communiqué looking for one particular word, and at last I found it: Kansas. Uncle Henry's Farm had been taken over. A mixture of sadness and anger swept over me. I felt hot all over and my eyes misted so that I was unable to finish reading the release. With trembling hands I took out my cell phone and rang the number that I knew so well to talk to Henry Baum.

There was no answer at first, but I persisted. I called five times, leaving messages on the answering machine. I decided to try to take it easy, obviously this was a sad day for him, he would need time to think about the changes and his future. But my thoughts were focusing in on just one individual, Mrs. West.

I recall that just at that moment I had but two thoughts in my head. One was to call the finance manager and tell her that I was willing to abandon my aspirations in exchange for the freedom of Henry's company. But remembering what he had said to me most definitely caused me to go for the second option. I had to take control of Oz once and for all, as then I would be able to return the control of his company to him. The situation was now no longer a professional matter – the battle had become personal.

The meeting that afternoon with Mugatu Design was a real success. Although they were not totally certain that the campaign as we offered it could succeed, they were willing to risk it and showed their faith, as they put it in their own words, "the team which created the best campaign of the decade", by which they meant the butterflies. Their own campaign would have a greater impact. I really needed it to.

As we drove back, Lionel, who had come with me and Oscar to the meeting, asked:

"What's up? You ought to be very pleased."

"I know, Lionel, but I can't get Henry out of my head."

"Listen, did you manage to speak to him?"

"No. I've called the office a number of times, his home, including his cell, and there's still no reply. I really hope nothing's happened."

"Like what?" Oscar asked from the back seat.

"I don't know. That company was his life. And it scares me to think…"

"Hold it right there, Dorothy," Lionel interrupted. "I can't believe my ears. What about looking for tangible information and staying out of the way of uncertainty? What was all that about? It was you who taught me to be courageous and to face up to my fears. Or doesn't that count for you?"

"Of course it does, Lionel, but it's so difficult…" I trailed off.

"Oh, I get it. So your problem is more serious than mine, right?"

"No Lionel, it's not that. I'm well aware of the fact that we mustn't judge the problems of others because although to us they seem small and easily solved, to the people involved they are real brick walls that seem impossible to get over. But when you're experiencing on of those problems under your own skin, well, it's just that much more difficult, right?"

"It shouldn't be. Suppose that someone you love is experiencing that situation. What would you say?" Oscar put it to me.

"Well, I'd say, stay cool, and that the last time I was talking with them, they seemed to have the situation under control. That's what I'd say."

"And then?" asked Lionel.

"You know it already. Try to dispel uncertainty, gather all the information you can on the subject, look for tangible facts…"

"And try to find some emotional support, right?"

"That's right, Lionel, and get some positive reinforcement." I looked up to find that as I drove on my blond friend had a smile on his lips.

"Hi, Dorothy, my name's Lionel and I'm your friend, you know you can count on me for anything you need…"

"Right, right!" I felt courage returning. "I see you learn fast."

"We're a great team, Ginger," said Oscar, "and we will not permit you to become down-hearted. We've just jumped the last hurdle and we should be feeling good about it."

"Okay guys, you're right. It's a fact that Henry has the necessary resources to get out of this situation. He will have heard my calls, listened to my messages, and when the time is right, he'll call me. Let's have a drink at Blue Note to celebrate Mugatu."

"Right on," put in Lionel. "It will give you a chance to tell us something more about yourself."

"That's right, it will be so interesting to find out a little more about your personal life." Oscar smiled.

"Take it easy, guys, I'm starting to worry you'll be giving me the third degree! Anyhow, I have to make a couple of calls first. Tim?" I said to my cell phone. "Everything has turned out okay and the guys and I are on the way to Blue Note to celebrate. Coming?… Great, we'll see you there."

The second call was to Boq, to tell him to put the machinery in motion. "Reach for the Stars" had begun.

Laughter, good music and pleasant conversation. That pretty much sums up the next episode. It felt so good to know that I could count on unconditional support. Tuesday was approaching and my courage was returning.

When I was rested I started to realise that Mrs. West's intention was to display her successes, so that mine would be cast in the shade. What happened on Monday had not been a personal attack, but rather just one more move in her campaign to seize the presidency. She wanted people to hold on to what was certain, stability and a share in economic power. People may get excited about a motivational project such as those I represented, but as a general rule, and even more so during a period of financial crisis, it's money that matters.

On the Tuesday, in keeping with her standard strategy, she informed the press of the financial status of the company. She had managed to multiply the profits by three, reduce the debt by half and optimise resources. Her figures were certainly very impressive. She was very good.

"Dorothy, excuse me."

"What is it, Boq?"

"What are we waiting for to raise some kind of opposition to her strength?"

"You can be very sure that Mrs. West is not going to make it easy. However, we must work and stay faithful to our initial plan. We already knew that she was going to try this. We must not react to her provocation. The final result is important, of course, but she has revealed her manoeuvre. We have to know how to use her strength against her."

"How do we do that?"

"Our team must concentrate on getting a million copies pasted up tonight. Wednesday we begin to implement our strategy."

"And in the meantime?"

"We shall have to put up with the side bets and try to move them onto our side. Tell Lionel that I want to hold a press conference tomorrow."

"That's more like it. Time for action!"

I rang Miss Toto.

"Good morning, how are you?"

"Ready for Friday, if a bit nervous."

"Just stay cool and remember what we talked about."

"Don't worry, everything is under control."

"What's the atmosphere among the staff?" I asked.

"It's heating up. There's a growing gap between the supporters of a more profitable, secure company and those who're backing the dream you are offering."

"Perfect. Thanks for everything, Toto."

"No need. But just one thing – do you really think it's good that people are dividing into two groups?"

"Yes, because as long as the split is appearing because some people are just thinking about profitability and security, Mrs. West strength will transform itself into her heaviest burden. That's the card we're playing."

"I feel better just listening to you, Dorothy. If you need me, you know where to find me. And don't worry about Friday."

"Thanks again, you're a sweetheart."

I then received the most important call of that week, and it wasn't about the absent Henry, it was Oscar Crow on the line.

"Dorothy, success! The simulator test worked beautifully. Everything is ready."

"Did you run tests under a variety of circumstances?"

"Of course. There's nothing to worry about. If conditions are as they're forecast to be, the effect will be perfect."

"I'm so pleased to hear you say that, Oscar. Thanks for all the good work."

I went back to controlling the situation. Having everything checked out was vital for my certainty and confidence. Everything seemed to be in place.

The rest of the day ran fairly smoothly, and consisted of meetings with the various departments to explain my proposals, deal with the rest of the managers involved and take account of their expectations, and above all a revision of the company financial data. Good preparation was crucial if I was to win out on Friday.

At three in the morning a text message came through to my cell phone. "Congratulations. Your footprint is all over NY".

When I got up on Wednesday and walked to the office I had the pleasure of seeing the invasion of the footprint all over the city. The central streets and the huge avenues near the most iconic parks were completed papered over with the black and white photo image. Public telephones, mail boxes, even some shop owners had given permission for their display windows to be used for the "Reach for the Stars" poster. You could read it everywhere, through the taxi windscreen, from the bus stops. Everybody was stopping to try and read the poster, and it looked from the way they reacted that they were pleased with what they saw, once they realised what it meant.

The call came from Mugatu very quickly. They were delighted, a number of news media had called to ask them about the campaign and the unlikely form of distribution. They took my advice and told the media that they would talk about it with them on Thursday.

I felt delighted that everything was turning out so well, but even more delighted when I turned on my computer and say that there was a message from Henry in the in-tray.

Dear Freckles,

I do apologise for not being able to contact you. Don't worry about a thing. Everything is under control. I guess the news of the takeover will have worried you, but you have to believe me when I say that the situation is better than you think. Soon we'll talk and I'll explain everything.

What about you? How's the tigon going? Have you tamed it yet?

I look forward to seeing you soon. You have my very best wishes for the general meeting on Friday, of course. Whatever happens, and whatever you see there, just don't lose sight of your objective.

Hugs,

Henry Baum

The day was turning out magnificently. Now my only concern was my campaign and it was time to take action. Lionel had the press conference ready. The entire staff were waiting to hear what I had to say.

"My dear colleagues," I said into the press microphone, "as you know, the Oz Company annual general meeting will be held on Friday. At that meeting, in view of the unexpected exit of Frank Wizard as President, there will be two candidates for the presidency of the company, and I am one of them. I am taking advantage of your presence here to tell you that the whole of my project and vision for the company will be set out and explained in detail to you all and to the investors on the day of the annual general meeting. Years ago this company based its action on the concept that greatness lies in simple ideas, but on Friday the company will be undergoing its own natural development, with new inspiration and a fresh development project involving everybody who works or collaborates with Oz Company. This new philosophy can be summed up in a new slogan: 'It's simple – we work magic.' Thank you all very much. I trust that at the meeting you will all take away a little of that magic."

Various media representatives tried to draw more information from me off the record, but sticking to Lionel's guidelines, I stayed in control of the situation.

Today the media victory, tomorrow the final day. How was Mrs. West intending to surprise me? I would soon find out.

That Thursday I checked the newspapers. Several made references to the press conference, but all talked about the strange and attractive Mugatu campaign. The financial papers that morning were talking about a new way to advertise, and praised my team to the skies for having followed the "Butterflies" campaign with "Reach for the Stars". Surprising, original and ingenious were the terms most used, but I never imagined that one of the regular reporters was going to introduce me to a new concept: extremely profitable.

Lionel, Tim and Oscar were waiting for me in the office. After a brief summary of the situation, they asked:

"Is everything ready?"

"As far as I'm concerned, it is," I replied. "The interview with Mr. Mugatu will be in the papers tomorrow, and my contribution to the general meeting is ready. I think we have sowed the seed of change. Now we have to water it."

"I, too, have everything ready," said Oscar. "Tim will help me tomorrow with the final execution."

"Yes, but don't forget that my team is exhausted after last night's bill posting marathon. That's a million posters, and while the result has been more than satisfactory, they now need some rest."

"Don't worry, Tim," I calmed his fears. "Your people will get all the rest they want tomorrow. But we'll need them in the entrance hall at ten o'clock tonight."

"No problem there, they're informed. They've been waiting for this day for weeks, and they aren't about to miss it now. Do you have everything tied up, Lionel?"

"Yes, Tim. The press has been invited, and I've already leaked the line that this will not only be an important meeting from an in-house point of view, but that we're going to reveal a revolutionary new device in the world of advertising. Everybody who witnessed "Butterflies" is sure not to miss it, and those who didn't won't want to have to go back to their editors with excuses. A massive turnout is guaranteed. The press room is prepared with everything they need to do their job to perfection."

"Excellent, gentlemen. Before we go, let me thank you again for your support and professionalism. Tomorrow will be a big day for this company and for us. I could never have imagined when I came into this emerald building for the first time just three months ago that now I would find myself in this situation. I couldn't have done it without you. Thank you."

"Dorothy, I think I speak for all of my companions when I say that it is we who should be thanking you. You gave us strength to be able to believe in change, and we had spent years just being dragged along by the current. You were the floating log we managed to grab hold of. As you say, tomorrow is an important day. But it's important because of the situation you have brought about. If you had not acted as you did, Mrs. West would have grabbed power. At least now we all have a chance."

As Tim fell silent, all four of us embraced each other firmly. This was a very powerful union.

We decided to go home and rest so that we would be fresh for the following day. When the guys had gone home, and I was just on the point of leaving the office, a voice from the couch in the centre took me by surprise.

" 'It's simple, we work magic.' A pretty line."

"Mrs. West?"

"Yes, my child, I was just coming to wish you luck for tomorrow. After all, whatever happens, we shall still be colleagues after the general meeting. You've been able to re-group and gain advantage from very complicated situations, you've adapted to situations so that they benefit you. You remind me very much of myself when I first arrived at this company..."

"What are you talking about?" I asked incredulously.

"When I was hired by Oz I had been running the finance department of a big fashion magazine. I had a lot of ambition and spirit, I was the happiest woman in the world. But it wasn't long before Frank disappeared, and little by little we realised that there was no-one at the helm, and I felt it incumbent upon me to take a more managerial role. I believed in the project, and I knew that if nobody did anything, it would founder, so I set out to buttress the financial position of the company."

"Very sensible, but..."

"Let me finish. The rest of the board went along with me, the members relaxed when they knew that I was steering and controlling everything. And little by little, they stopped performing their directorial duties. I felt frustrated and isolated. There was nobody to support me during those difficult times. And as you know, I managed to keep the project afloat and turn it into the largest business in its field in this country. I can't understand why people now raise their eyebrows because I'm merely officially claiming the position which I've been doing for years under cover, as you might say."

"I understand how you are bound to feel, Mrs. West, but did it occur to you that there might be other ways of running the company? It's evident that the staff don't support you because they don't agree with the way you do things."

"There is no other way! They had to leave the power in my hands for the thing to work. Where there is a power vacuum, someone must take the reins."

"I'm not passing judgement on your decisions, merely trying to make you see that you were wrong on the method. Fear is a powerful ally, but an amazing creator of enemies. I believe in bringing the teams together, in motivation and inspiration, in getting everybody involved in the success which surrounds us. If I have a dream, I want them to be able to enjoy it."

Mrs. West was silent for a few moments, then raised her eyes to mine and turning to leave, she said:

"The best of luck for tomorrow, Dorothy. But I am merely claiming what is rightfully mine."

16

The Invisible Magician

"We cannot solve problems by thinking in the same
way as we did when we created them"

Albert Einstein

Mrs. West's words were still echoing in my head when Friday dawned and I was once again entering the fabulous emerald Oz Company building. I would never have believed that Mrs. West could have revealed herself to be so vulnerable. There was no escaping the fact that that her reasoning was based on common sense. If you see that something dear to you is beginning to sink, it's natural for you to try to take the helm and keep it afloat. I have no idea how I would feel if I had performed a great task for the company and then somebody else showed up to reap the rewards.

Sometimes we fail to consider the situation of the people in front of us or even with whom we share our daily lives. If we're in a good mood, we almost oblige everybody around us to be in a similar mood, and if we're sad and downcast, it can even be irritating to find someone bathed in happiness. We should try to understand and be concerned so as to discover the personal situations of those around us, so that we can better understand their reactions, expectations and ambitions.

I believe that Mrs. West was wrong to try to replace Frank Wizard by means of such a strict policy, but, obviously, who would have taken any notice of her if she had not acted in that way? If I had been in that situation, would I have been able to master it?

The elevator had not yet arrived when a soft voice woke me from my musings.

This could be the most decisive day of the year for you. You look as if you're miles away.

"Good morning , Miss North, excuse me. How are you?"

"Optimistic. Everything has worked out the way you said it would. Today Mugatu Design is in all the media. They're talking about how simple, immediate, original and profitable the campaign has turned out to be. 'A simple campaign, run by the most talented team in the country, to be rounded off by a special delight tonight'," she read from the newspaper she was carrying.

"That's marvellous, the investors will bear tonight in mind when they vote."

"You seem a little sad, Dorothy. Is there something on your mind?"

"I'm not sure. Yesterday just as I was leaving Mrs. West came to see me."

"Really? What did she want? Was she suggesting you withdraw? Or perhaps share the presidency?"

"No, Heidi. She just wished me luck for today. She told me what the situation was like when she began to assume power, and the fact is that it has given me a lot to think about."

"Oh, she is very good," Heidi smiled.

"How do you mean?" I didn't understand.

"I'm not saying that what she told you isn't true. As you know, I was with the company during that period, and there's no doubt that things were starting to slip. There were a number of months of uncertainty until quite surprisingly Frank, or perhaps someone pretending to be him, brought back some degree of stability. Nobody can deny Mrs. West's importance at that time. But the current situation is different. The scenario we face involves a person who has turned her back on creativity, inspiration and interest in the products, and is focusing only on profitability. You cannot use the past to justify an unfortunate vision of the future. You represent that return to the values which motivated us and made us feel proud to be involved in a great project. You're keeping the spirit of Frank Wizard alive."

"I understand that, Heidi, but... Why do you say that she's good? I still don't get it."

"It's simple. She knows that you are the kind of person who never ignores what people say or remark. You like to actively listen to, and try to understand people. She is aware of your empathy and your human qualities. So, naturally, she has used what you would see as your strengths to create doubt in yourself. She knew that if she gave you a coherent and emotional explanation, you would begin to think of other possibilities and you would justify her actions. You would be weaker and would fail to provide a staunch defence of your position when you faced her tonight."

"She even said I reminded her of herself..."

"Of course! So you saw in her a person you did not wish to become and you doubted whether you were doing the right thing. You have to admit, she is very good."

After thinking it over for a few seconds I was forced to smile and accept what Heidi North was trying to tell me. What I thought I could do to her with the financial data, she had succeeded in doing with me by social skills. Without eliminating the past and its possible justification, it was obvious that Mrs. West knew what she was doing. She had revealed that her intelligence was more powerful than mine. A good thing that my team was supporting and backing me.

"You are absolutely right, Heidi! She managed to deactivate me for quite a number of hours, and if I had not spoken to you, she would certainly have achieved her goal. I must check that everything is in order and prepared. I'll see you tonight at the general meeting."

"I'll be there!" and Heidi hurried away across the entrance hall.

I entered the elevator and pressed the button for floor thirty. I would begin on the higher floors, so that the first person I would see would be Lionel. I needed to check that everything was ready and that the news media had been lined up.

"So, is everything ready?"

"Yes, Dorothy, as I told you yesterday, everyone has been informed. My team is now fixing up the communications equipment in the hall and connecting the internal television signal to the panels in the entrance hall. All the staff will be able to follow the general meeting from there."

"Nice work, Lionel. Tonight is going to be magic."

"I'm ready to tackle anybody I have to. We have to be prepared to put up a strong defence against anybody who tries to water down our message."

"And if they do?"

"It's simple, we work magic," he replied with a huge smile.

I then went down to floor twenty and walked into Tim's metal room. It was completely empty, all the staff taking a rest after the bill posting night.

"Good morning, Tim."

"Hi Ginger. Are you ready?"

"Yes, I can't wait for this evening to come. Is everything ready at your end?"

"Naturally, Oscar and I have done a great deal of work, but I think it was worth it. You'll soon see."

"I'm sure of it. I'm in your hands."

After leaving Tim, I paused on floor seventeen. Although I had seen it a number of times I was always amazed to see such innovative equipment in that room. I stood for a moment looking at the plants which Oscar had kept so he could continue his experiments.

"This was where it began," said Oscar, appearing from behind one of the smoke screens.

"They will always be special for me."

"For me, too, for sure. We must never forget that it was thanks to the plants that we regained our lost inspiration and enthusiasm."

"It seems like a long time ago now, doesn't it? The pace of these weeks has been exhausting."

"It may be so, but when you work with motivation and a belief in the objective, the job becomes much more fun. I've really enjoyed these weeks."

"Well get yourself ready, because if we succeed tonight, you'll have no chance to stop working," I told him.

"I hope so, Dorothy. The brain stays young if it's always working and creating."

"Is everything ready?"

"Perfectly ready. Tim has been enormously generous with his time and company. It's been a pleasure to be able to work with him over these days. He's a great guy."

"I'm delighted to hear it."

Thrilled to see my friends in this mood, I went down to floor twelve to my office. A burst of applause from my colleagues surprised me. It was really exciting to see to room so full of life and affection. Everybody had worked so hard on the recent campaigns and they had strengthened me and supported me on my personal project. I simply had to clap them too.

"But don't forget that the important bit is still to come. We mustn't rest on our laurels. Tonight we shall have a real victory to celebrate."

I sat down at my desk, noticing how my team was ready to set to work with a will and enthusiasm. This was the Oz spirit, or at least the one I wanted for the company.

"Today we sent the email to everybody, staff, clients, collaborators and suppliers."

"Excellent, Boq, thanks! How did it go?"

"According to the information we have, it simply says 'the magic starts tonight', and then moves on to the company logo and says the time: eleven pm."

"Excellent. What's been the reaction?"

"Judging by the press conference on Wednesday and the repercussions in the press yesterday, the Mugatu Design campaign and particularly the interview with Mr. Mugatu which comes out today in the most important media outlets in the sector, we think everybody is on the edge of their seats. Everybody is waiting to see how you'll surprise us this time."

"And the staff?"

"As Miss Toto says, everybody is excited about our proposal, but some are betting on economic security as represented by Mrs. West."

What Boq said really gave me heart, and as I walked home to get ready for the big occasion, I mentally went over what this situation meant.

That night everything was going to change, so I had better look my absolute best, and make sure the image I projected was as positive as possible. Whether we like it or not, our image is of the utmost importance, so we had better stop being slaves to it and transform it into our best ally. A relaxing shower, moisturiser and understated makeup. Pink and mauve tones had always done a good job in bringing out my green eyes.

I decided to wear my hair up with chopsticks, since I knew that this projected a young and casual look. As my dress, I chose a white kimono picked out in red, an outfit which certainly projected originality and staying power. The small red handbag was a comfortable accessory for the symbol which all my colleagues were hoping to see. The start of all the movement for change - the fantastic red Mugatu shoes.

Checking myself in the mirror, I was quite surprised to see how good I looked. I smiled into the mirror and drew strength from a quotation which someone once told me: "Put your future in the best hands – yours".

I arrived at nine-thirty in a taxi at the doors of the wonderful building. In half an hour the general meeting would open. Oscar was wearing a great suit the colour of ripe maize, with a brown Mao shirt, while Tim was wearing an excellently cut grey suit with a sky blue tie. Lionel was in a striking dark amber Windsor cut suit, with a white shirt and an ochre tie. When they saw me, they all came up to the taxi, smiling.

"Unreal, Ginger, you look fantastic!" remarked Lionel.

"You all look great. We should dress like this more often." I was on a high.

"Remind me to tell you that when this pair aren't listening, I want to marry you." Tim was in a fantastic mood.

"What? I don't think I'm your type, but thanks, Tim, that's praise coming from you."

"Shall we work a little magic?" Oscar asked to give me courage.

"Let's work magic!" I answered firmly, as we moved towards the door.

"Just one moment, Dorothy," Lionel's face was serious. "Before you go in, you have to be prepared. Take a deep breath and think about everything that's waiting for you on the other side of these doors. Enjoy it and have a good time. You deserve it. Ah, and have one of these," he passed me a tissue. "I hope you won't need it, but…"

As he spoke, Tim and Oscar opened the enormous entrance door. In the building hundreds of people were beginning to congratulate us and clap. Cheers could be heard from all sides. I picked out Toto, Boq and my team, the members of my companions' teams and there were dozens of others I had never spoken to. All were excitedly supporting our candidature. The huge screens showed my face, my eyes misty with emotion.

Just before we reached the yellow elevator, I turned around, and everybody fell silent, waiting for me to say something.

"Tonight we're going to do something great. I hope I'll always be able to count on the support you're giving me today. I promise I'll never let you down. This company must be delighted to employ workers like you, capable of such inspiration and able to motivate others. I thank you all."

The room exploded with cheers. All eyes and smiles were on our little group, some pressing my companions' hands, encouraging us and wishing us luck.

When we reached the elevator the man with the cute moustache waved us through. The yellow tiles looked more brilliant than ever. Before we began the ascent, the elevator operator handed me a mysterious envelope.

"What is it?" I asked.

"They left it for you. It's important," he answered as the doors began to close.

"That's weird!" said Oscar. "What could it be?"

I replied as I looked for the signature, "It's a letter from Uncle Henry!"

I could hardly contain my happiness and surprise as I rapidly read the letter.

Dear Freckles,

Today you have triumphed. Only a few months ago you travelled to a new city, to a new company, burdened with uncertainty and doubt, and look at you now! You're surrounded by the best professionals in the business, you run some amazing campaigns and you're just about to reach a new milestone. My congratulations. Whatever happens at the general meeting, today you have triumphed.

Shortly before you left I told you the story about the tigon and I now see that you have not only found your own, but you have transformed it into a mischievous baby that purrs at your orders. Congratulations.

I also said on that day that if you achieved a great deed, I would tell you my greatest secret: the story of the invisible magician. You have done better than my wildest dreams, so here it is. I hope you like it, and that it brings you luck.

The story goes that a young magician, having arrived from a distant land, set up his home in a community called BigMapple. Living in his ancient villa, the young man, whose name was Sullivan, excited and amazed his neighbours with his tricks and illusions. He could put himself into a tiny bottle, or make flowers grow out of a rock. He made the birds speak and fish walk on land. His deeds always excited enormous anticipation, so he decided to try his luck in the huge neighbouring city.

When he arrived there, however, he found something entirely unexpected. He went everywhere looking for a break, but it appeared that if you weren't called Merlin, Copperfield or Houdini, nobody would let you so much as pull a rabbit out of a hat. They told him to come back later, that the list was full, or that the mood of the times didn't like magicians.

Many days passed while Sullivan tried to demonstrate his talent, and it just got harder and harder to find an open door. His need to earn some money and the drive to score a success finally led him to take a crucial decision. If everyone wanted a great magician, he would give them what they wanted. After practising some new tricks for a few days, he made himself an enormous cloak and a powerful hat. A few days later his chance came. Ana, the ancient wise woman of the lake, had decided to hire a magician for her show.

Dozens of magicians turned up to apply: illusionists and escapologists, magicians specialising in cards and string – there was even one whose assistant was a frog. But when his turn came, the young magician refused to be put off. He fluttered his cloak and began to tell a series of tales which were, no doubt, exaggerations of his actual experiences. Everybody there was impressed by the deeds he talked about, his fantastic clothing and magic hat.

Ana listened carefully to the reactions of the audience, and when they were quiet she asked Sullivan to do a trick.

The young magician waved his hands and to everybody's amazement transformed all the horses into English gentlemen and all the English gentlemen into amusing squirrels in evening dress. He made a nearby tree light up with coloured bulbs and made all the houses round about rise two metres into the air. Ana was unmoved by these tricks, and only when they heard the final applause did she smile. "You're hired", she said.

During the following weeks he played his part to perfection, performing all his magic and putting on some splendid shows. His fame spread like dust on the wind and all the people of BigMapple queued up to enjoy his magic. The young magician was delighted because he was doing what he liked best, and Ana treated him like a real magical genius.

But one thing bothered him every night when he finished the show, a niggling irritation which caused a doubt to take shape. He was unsure whether the success was really his or did it belong to the person he had invented. He felt like a confidence trickster, a cheat, and because the old lady treated him so well, one day, taking advantage of the shadows of the night, he disappeared.

Sullivan wandered from place to place, performing in other towns, and put on many successful performances, but he was unable to free himself of the unease he felt within himself. One day he realised that he would have to return to BigMapple and make his peace with Ana. He would have to tell her the truth. After all, she had always treated him well.

He appeared before the old lady without his cloak and proceeded to explain himself:

"My dear Ana, my name is Sullivan and I am not the great magician I once told you I was. Faced with rejection and never getting a break, I had to create a disguise, and this has weighed increasingly heavily on me as time has gone by. I made myself a wonderful cloak and a marvellous hat and passed myself off as a great illusionist. In this way I got you to offer me work, but ever since then I have become more and more unhappy. I'm sorry I lied to you, but I had no other option, I hope you can understand and that one day you will forgive me".

The old lady thought for a moment, then replied:

"My dear Sullivan, you are the person who made coloured light bulbs appear in the trees, made the houses levitate and performed other wonders. So on one matter you are wrong, you devoted so much time to creating the disguise you have mentioned that in the end you really became that great magician. But you put so much effort into deceiving

me that you missed one important detail. Your wonderful cloak and your marvellous hat meant nothing to me, because I, my dear Sullivan, am blind".

I thought I had no other option and I really was blind.

Henry Baum

17

The Balloon Journey

"Success means obtaining your desires.
Happiness, enjoying what you have obtained"

Ralph Waldo Emerson

When I reached the fifty-seventh floor and the elevator door opened, the scene that met my eyes left me petrified. The area in which the chairs were arranged was completely full of people, every one of whom was studying us. Some smiled, some greeted us amiably.

"So you're the famous redhead," said one. "Congratulations on your work. Your campaigns are the best we've seen in recent times. This is the most reliable demonstration of the fact that fresh air is blowing through the company."

I thanked him for his words, realising that his group of serious-looking people would be some of the investors so feared by the defenders of a motivated and inspired company.

We moved into the plenary meeting room, now looking very different from how it had done a few days before. Everything was fully lit and decorated with the Oz Company corporate icon. Huge banners with the logo decorated the aisles and stage. The huge windows which surrounded the room provided an amazing panorama of New York on a clear night with a huge full moon, looking like a great observer and judge of the general meeting.

As we moved towards the front row I felt that I was being minutely observed by the dozens of investors who had now taken their seats. We climbed the four steps up to the stage and occupied our respective named seats. At that moment I felt like a small child, eating an ice cream in the park with my father, not because of the pleasure, but because of the feeling that I had so much to learn. My teeth immediately gripped my lower lip, so as I took my seat I struggled to keep calm.

Mombi, Monk and South were already waiting in their seats. While we waited for Heidi, West and Frank to appear, I decided to glance at the notes I was carrying.

"Any last minute advice?" I asked my companions.

"Stay calm and enjoy yourself. Nobody can feel that you don't deserve this job. Explain your ideas clearly and simply, in short, user-friendly sentences."

"I'll do my best, but I'm feeling pretty nervous…"

"As Oscar says, you don't have to worry about these people. This isn't an exam. You have reached the hearts of millions with your campaigns and they have benefited financially. That was your exam. All you have to do now is explain your thoughts about the future of the company. Get them to share your vision," said Tim.

"And if Mrs. West attacks me?"

"Your wit will be your ally," replied Oscar.

"Anyway, be a scratched record. Repeat your power ideas and don't change the basis of your message. Change the way you explain it and offer new ways of approaching it, but don't alter your objective." Tim added in support.

"It's also important to find weaknesses in their speech, so you can stop on something that puts you in the right. That will make it look as though the whole of your speech is right."

"What's that technique called?"

"They call it the smoke screen, but that doesn't matter. Remember: sentences they can't disagree with."

"One more thing," put in Lionel. "Always be positive, offer them small and exciting successes and a solid future."

"You're a perfect team, guys."

"We are, Ginger, we are," said Lionel.

While my blond friend was saying that, I was watching the last investors taking their seats, and from the central doors I could make out the figures of Heidi North and Mrs. West making their appearance. The former was wearing a pearl grey figure-hugging suit, silver shoes and she had a white scarf at her throat. She was a few metres ahead of Mrs. West.

When she made her appearance several investors hurried to greet her and I noticed that their approach was quite respectful. She was wearing an interesting red and black dress looking like two handkerchiefs crossing over each other ending up in the shape of a tube to the knee. Stylish black Mugatu shoes completed the ensemble. She was, as always, fantastic.

When they had taken their seats the lights of the hall dimmed and the huge screen at our back began to show a promotional video about the company. A speaker described the great campaigns and successes which the company had created during its life. It showed many scenes which were fixed in our memories: polar bears, the inflatable doll, the cheeky lime and lemon cartoon, and so on, all ending with the Oz logo and a line which the speaker intoned with a degree of solemnity:

> "We offer a well-deserved welcome to the creator of so many successes, a person able to satisfy our dreams and expectations, to this, which will be his final general meeting as President of Oz Company...let's give a warm welcome to ... Frank Wizard!"

Everybody present stood up and wildly clapped the person who was coming in from the yellow elevator in the centre of the hall. The investors seated at the sides of the central aisle jumped out of their seats to greet him personally and shake his hand. All my companions on the board of directors were smiling and clapping wildly.

As for me, I felt an enormous wave of heat take over my whole body, I was so moved. All I could see was a perfectly fitting black suit and carefully brushed greying hair. Frank's hands were waving at the crowd, still grasping those of the people who wanted to greet him. As he made his way to the foot of the stage I began to think that I might know who he was. All that had been needed was his appearance, and now he had appeared, the reference point, the icon, the totem... Henry Baum!

My whole body was shaking when, having climbed the final steps of the stage, his gentle blue eyes locked on mine with a huge smile, and as he moved by my side he placed his hand on my shoulder and said: "I'm the invisible magician, Freckles. I'm proud of you."

Now I understood everything. His repeated absences from the Farm, his exhausting marathon days, how hard it was to locate him sometimes and now the apparent calm with which he talked about what Oz was doing. My feelings were in turmoil, I had no idea how to behave. Scores of questions pounded in my brain – what should I do, what was I supposed to think?

Suddenly I caught sight of something even more astounding if that were possible. I could see a supportive expression from a few places along the table, a friendly face with lips which said: "Take it easy, you're doing fine." It wasn't the warm empathy that left me stunned. It was the fact that the message was being transmitted from the perfectly chiselled lips of Mrs. West.

I turned my face to the floor and said to myself: "There is an explanation for all this, I must not let myself be carried away by my feelings. I must remove myself from everything which stands between me and my objective. I must be focused and achieve what we have intended to achieve. I must not be bothered by external noise. All in good time I shall understand everything".

"Everything okay, Ginger?" Tim asked.

"Don't worry, I'm great. My nerves gave me a bit of a shock, but I'm back under control."

"Do you want me to ask for a break?"

"No, really. Everything's fine."

Henry took his place before the microphone and began his speech. Perplexed as I was by the situation, I tried to pay careful attention, to attempt to decipher something from what he had to say which would provide me with a satisfactory answer.

"My dearest friends. This is a very important day for me. It's more than thirty years ago now that I founded this great company. Thirty years of good times, big successes, but above all of the good people who have come with me. We cut our teeth with small campaigns for local shopkeepers. Adolescence arrived almost without our noticing it, with some national companies who hired us, let's be honest, because we had good ideas and weren't expensive," he said amid the laughter.

"But it was barely a dozen years ago, in the dawn of the spread of the internet, that, thanks to the faith of Singular Globe, Oz Company came of age. As the video shows, a lot of great companies have passed through our hands. Their faith has been our spur. We've worked hard to become what we are: the major marketing company in the land."

A round of applause drowned his words.

"But today we face a whole new situation. We never wanted to believe that it was coming, but the fact is, it's here. Our company is in the third age. Many of you have helped me from the beginning, and have tried to convince me to carry on the project. But you all know what I'm like – I will never hold onto a position that I think should belong to somebody else. And that time has come.

"Today you're confronted with two choices of leader. W. West represents stability at a time when it appears as if the world economy is waking up with a hangover resulting from to many parties in the past. She's hard working, very demanding, and her focus on results is worthy of the world's best number crunchers. Her strategy is clearly defined and her professional experience boosts her application for the job. I wish you the best of luck, Wendy!"

Again, everybody started to clap.

"But as always in this company, there's an ace lurking up someone's sleeve. The name of that ace is Dorothy Grimm. Many of you don't know her, but she's responsible for "Butterflies" and "Reach for the Stars", she's tenacious and untiring, ingenious and resolute. She has given us back the inspiration which the company had and has made us believe that Oz Company can get back to the garden. Both offers are good enough for me to feel comfortable about retiring, and I am quite certain that whoever you vote for today will take our company to new heights previously undreamed of.

"All I want to say to these two is that after today, I beg you to join forces. A company such as ours cannot afford to lose any of the assets you represent. Good luck!" he concluded looking at us both, while the audience broke out once again into applause.

"Don't go!" cried out one of the investors.

"Of course, I never shall. This is my home, my soul. Whatever happens, there will always be a part of me within these emerald walls. I have spent my best years at your side. That's why, because I know that you will respect the decision of this evening's vote, and because I know that with you my dream will outlast my physical body, I give you my thanks.

"Thank you, each and every one of you, past, present and future members of the company for your talent and time. Thanks to the members of the board for supporting me and making it possible for us to proceed with a clear and successful course set. And thanks to Wendy West and Dorothy Grimm, for showing me that I leave Oz Company in good hands."

The din caused by the cheering and clapping was deafening. There were several minutes with the entire audience on their feet, not a few tears and a deeply moved Henry were the outcome of such an emotional speech.

The next few minutes flew by. The meeting stewards provided everybody present with a folder in which they could read all the data about the candidatures. What I remember about that was that Mrs. West's presentation was spectacular. Graphs, percentages, and development background charts. All the economic groundwork for the audience to make themselves thoroughly convinced at a glance of the great developments that the company had undergone. Just half an hour later, and she was on. She rose, walked to the microphone, and after a brief introduction, welcome and thanks, she reached the kernel of her speech.

"So, then, it's clear that the financial situation of the company has reached levels of historic prosperity. We have generated more income than at any other time in the company's history. And thanks to the mergers we have made with the most representative companies of the twenty most powerful states in the country, Oz Company is now a significant point of reference. Everybody respects us. This means that we are the best product, the most sought after, and the one which give the clients most peace of mind. With us, they know that everything will turn out well, that their campaigns will be effective and that they have a solvent, effective and serious backer.

"But that is only our initial objective. In the future I would like to have the opportunity of addressing you, as Frank has just done, to tell you that we have become a world icon, a symbol of prosperity, of reliability and of the profitability of our ideas."

In between the outbursts of clapping from the audience, Mrs. West concluded her speech by emphasising her wish and commitment to increase the investors' incomes and the stability of all the staff.

"If you give me your trust, I shall continue to show you that I am capable of attaining my objectives", was her concluding sentence. Following which, and while the applause continued even more loudly, if that were possible, Mrs. West resumed her seat with an enormous smile on her face.

It was my turn.

While I was getting up, Tim, Oscar and Lionel gave me their hands to encourage me. Henry looked at me, and said in a very low, but very sure voice: "Go to it, Ginger!" Mombi, South and Monk were already concentrating on my report.

"Good evening. Before I begin my statement, I would like to pass the microphone to a colleague whom you all certainly know. She stands closer to all the workers in the company, and that's why I would like you to hear her. This company is a vessel which would never arrive safely in port if we lacked motivated and inspired sailors. That's why I believe that we should all listen to her opinion on this matter before we continue. Please, pay attention to Miss Toto."

A murmur of voices was heard in the hall, while all heads turned to look at the young woman who was making her way with confident steps to my side. She was slightly nervous, but that passed as soon as she began to speak.

"If I were to ask the people present at this meeting about their aspirations and desires for the future, I am sure that ninety per cent of you would say that you wanted to be happy. All well and good, but that would not help us to define an overall objective, since what makes a person happy has absolutely nothing to do with what will make the person facing you happy. But something has changed in recent months, something tangible and real. For the majority of the company staff and myself, happiness is based on togetherness and collaboration between everybody, on an inspirational spirit and the knowledge of being a part of a project we can feel proud of. This would be a project in which the information girl can speak to the management without barriers, and all employees feel that they are being listened to. That would be happiness for any worker, and it is for us, too. It turns out that this dream is real, we have been experiencing and enjoying this spirit for weeks, and thanks to the express desire and opportunity Dorothy Grimm has given me, I feel able to speak to you all on behalf of the staff. I want you to help us keep the dream alive. No, more than that, I invite you to share that dream. Thank you."

Henry rose to his feet and began to clap. We all joined in, while Miss Toto left the stage and prepared to return to the entrance hall. She was blushing and her moist eyes were fixed on the floor as she made for the yellow elevator.

I returned to the microphone and went on with my strategy.

"Let's keep the dream alive. There is no doubt that we have just heard a very accurate observation for a day like today. My name is Dorothy Grimm and I want us all to recover our dreams, but at the cost of nothing.

"When I arrived at Oz Company I found myself in company with a group of professionals with enormous talent, but it was rusty or dormant. This is a waste of talent which a company such as ours cannot afford.

"There is no doubt that the work which Mrs. West has done as regards profitability and the expansion of the company has been very positive on paper, but it has revealed our worst instincts, casting aside the affectivity of our great professionals and projecting an image of pride and vanity. We all agree on the importance of increasing profits, but as we have seen, there are other ways to do this. I should like to be proud of having achieved my dreams through inspiration, motivation and imagination.

"We should strive to recover the basic standards which Frank instilled in the company, which have undoubtedly been enormously fruitful: communication, trust, coordination..."

"But these are outdated laws! They have no validity in a market such as the current one!" Mr. Monk interrupted my speech.

"The law of gravity is the oldest, yet it hasn't lost its validity, has it?"

The room burst out laughing while Monk remained completely frozen by my reaction.

"If we allow our professionals to seek their fortunes with other companies who can make use of them, we will certainly be losing the battle."

"I've taken part in a lot of campaigns, and I think I could do the jobs of quite a lot of people," muttered South.

"Dear Mrs. South, I like practising extreme winter sports, and I've broken a number of bones over the past few years, but that doesn't make me a broken bone specialist. Please, let's get real."

A slight outburst of clapping could be heard from the room amid the laughter of the audience.

"We must have faith in our projects and generate global ideas. This is the legacy and the idiosyncrasy of Oz Company. If we can rely on brilliant professionals we shall develop brilliant campaigns, and obviously they will generate higher profits, enhance the company's reputation and create that feeling of pride we were talking about before. Greatness lies in simple ideas, we must never forget it.

"With the 'Butterflies' campaign, we touched the hearts of the world. We spent less than half of the budget allocated for the previous campaign, we managed to achieve a greater impact and we generated a line of business previously non-existent. In these few weeks dozens of businesses have become interested in our famous plants, which is an innovative and revolutionary product which will generate unexpected profits for us. There is no doubt that it was a magnificent campaign which made use of a number of departments who stood shoulder to shoulder, and raised the banner of brilliance still higher. But it also demonstrated that a good idea may be the most effective way of generating profits."

While some of the investors applauded they remembered the campaign, another raised his voice and called out:

"But we are greater and stronger now!"

"And I'm sure that your ego is most satisfied," I laughed. "But my formula doesn't exclude that possibility. We have to think about continuing to grow, all the more if we are already great. But the growth must be in the hearts and minds of the clients and in the hearts of the consumers.

"As you know, we are now in the middle of launching the 'Reach for the Stars' campaign, a campaign which, once again, demonstrates an original, talent-based idea, which hits people much more effectively than any huge promotion requiring astronomical budgets. There are companies which only ever have one brilliant idea in the whole of their existence. Oz Company has had two in barely six months. This is how we show the competition that we are irresistible, but, still, if what you want is something more visual, signs with our name on them plastered all over the country…"

"We all agree that 'Butterflies' was a stroke of genius," Mr. Mombi interrupted me. "But it was a flash in the pan. 'Reach for the Stars' is a cheap campaign, lacking in originality. The image of a footprint outside the Chinese Theatre has been used until we are bored with it."

"What gives you the idea that that is all that the footprint represents?" came a voice from a perfectly suited silhouette at the back of the hall.

"Excuse me, who are you?" Mombi asked.

"A few days ago, Dorothy Grimm and her companions came to me to put that idea to me in person. I thought that it was fresh, original and moving. But the one thing that convinced me was this: they all believed in what they were telling me, and they managed to include me in their dream. My name is Giovanni Mugatu."

Amid the amazement of the audience and the press representatives who hurriedly started to take photographs, the famous designer began to move towards the stage, stopping when he reached my side.

"They asked me to hold a press conference," he went on, "to inform the public that today, Friday, the campaign would move into a second phase. They didn't tell me what it consisted of, but if the results of the first phase continue to be satisfactory, I cannot believe that whatever it is will fail. Here I am, Dorothy, work your magic on me." He smiled. "Oh, and by the way, great shoes!"

"Thank you, Mr. Mugatu. As I was saying, talent and brilliance are the best assets we have. This is the best way to show the competition that we are irresistible, but, as I say, if anyone requires something more visible, like signs with our logo on throughout the country... well, it's easy! Let's work some magic!"

At the precise moment I was saying that, Oscar operated the remote control, and from floor seventeen the huge apparatus which I thought looked like a telescope began to project on the beautiful face of the moon the famous photograph of the Mugatu footprint.

The people in the hall simply could not believe their eyes, and their jaws actually dropped. The famous photograph no longer represented the typical image of the imprint of the actors in Hollywood Boulevard, now it was a copy of the famous footprint left by Neil Armstrong on the moon. At last the whole thing made sense. The scene was spectacular. The huge windows surrounding the room revealed the incredible footprint. A huge Mugatu footprint, printed on the moon, dominating the sky, catching the stars.

The journalists' cameras started flashing and the investors began to applaud, stunned, while Giovanni Mugatu simply shed a tear.

"Today is a new day for advertising. Before us is a new horizon, and the talent in our team can conquer it. Let's keep on dreaming, let's work magic!" I brought my speech to a triumphant conclusion.

You could hear the cheers from the entrance hall, where every inch of space in the marvellous emerald room was packed with staff members. Henry Baum rose from his seat, unable to contain his excitement, his eyes wet with tears, and hugged me.

"Thanks for everything, Freckles. I knew I was right about you."

"But Henry…"

"When the proceedings are over, I'll explain everything."

I used the fact that everyone was still stunned with amazement to move over to my companions. The way I was smiling clearly indicated how I was feeling. I took all their hands and congratulated them, bathed in excitement for the way my presentation had turned out.

It took more than twenty minutes for everybody to get back to their seats, although even then people were staring incredulously at the moon, still unable to believe their eyes. After a few more questions from the investors, and replies from my colleagues, we moved on to considering the decision to be made. This took only a few minutes, and then came the terrible moment of the vote.

The first person to reveal his vote was Oscar, followed by Tim and Lionel supporting my candidature. As we had foreshadowed, the votes of Mr. Monk, Mrs. South and Mr. Mombi plus Mrs. West's own, meant that her own candidature had four votes. I, of course, voted for myself so the voting stood at a tie. Now we had the vote of Frank Wizard himself, and the double-weight votes of the investors to come. When they were ready to cast their votes, Henry stood up and said:

"I feel unable to decide between such imposing talents. In view of the fact that this is my last general meeting, I beg you to accept my abstention."

This didn't surprise me, so it meant that it would be the investor's vote which was decisive. This was the only way that his image could emerge untarnished from this battle. A new period would open without any blood being spilt. It was an intelligent move.

"Dear friends of Oz Company," the investors' spokesman began. "There is no doubt that we have been deeply moved and satisfied by the results obtained and the presentations produced by each candidate. Both guarantee a prosperous and profitable future.

However, in view of the current situation in the company, we are obliged to choose a candidate. It is for this reason, and counting on the fact that both professionals will be able to work together and create many successes together, the new President of Oz Company will be… Dorothy Grimm."

All I can recall of that explosion of joy is that Tim caught me up in his arms and threw me into the air, Lionel and Oscar were hugging each other and that Henry burst into tears on the podium.

It was a party, everybody was congratulating me, and I had never seen people so happy …

It was midnight, by which time almost all of our colleagues had gone off to the marvellous Shabay terrace to celebrate the outcome of the general meeting. Henry, who was still there in the great hall, asked me to come with him.

"The time has come to resolve all your doubts," he said.

We entered the incredible yellow elevator, and when he inserted a golden key, the elevator began to move up to the fifty-eighth floor.

18

Home Again

"Many people miss the small happinesses
watching out for the big one"

Pearl S. Buck

The doors opened as we reached the top floor of the building. The pleasant voice telling us that we had arrived had hardly fallen silent when my eyes fell on a scene I could hardly believe.

Floor fifty-eight was an office of around a hundred square metres with a broad and dominating desk, a rest area with chairs in the shape of eggs and a coffee table bearing a beautiful bonsai tree. Teak was the dominant colour of the furniture and of the columns which separated the glass sliding doors which opened onto a huge terrace.

The views were amazing. New York was at our feet. There were barely twenty buildings in the city as tall as ours. The lit-up offices were a real postcard view. The soft breeze blowing that night over the huge block seemed to expand still more the sense of space and feeling of peace.

"I guess you're a little confused," Henry began.

"There are so many things I don't understand…"

"Then I'll start at the beginning. I want you to be very clear about everything. Why don't we take a seat, out on the terrace?

"Everything started on arrival in this frantic city. As you would have understood when you read *The Invisible Magician,* at first nobody would give me a break so I decided to create the Frank Wizard character. Since the Kansas clients knew me and knew about the successful campaigns I'd run, I used these perceptions to explain that this man was a promising talent who'd learned with us and had created some inspired ideas. I even created the illusion that he left us when The Farm was having a hard time.

"The response was quick in coming and the first clients started to appear. Everything was working out perfectly and in a few short months requests for campaigns were rolling in."

"But that would bind you to this character, wouldn't it?"

"It did, but that was a minor problem. After all, I was doing what I wanted to do, working with clients and setting up a business in the Big Apple. You know that advertising has been my life. It made up for the sacrifice. People wouldn't recognise me because of my creations, but that gave me the chance to be able to create them. Not to mention the financial advantage, of course…"

"But that was the beginning of the problem, right?"

"Precisely. I felt that the company had to grow and be an advertising and marketing company which based its strength on creativity, inspiration, team work…"

"Greatness lies in simple ideas," I interjected.

"Ha, ha. One day I'll tell you how that line came up, but yes, that was the spirit. Unfortunately, I didn't realise that by asking investors to believe in my project, I was mortgaging that dream. Little by little they started to demand greater profitability, and of course, that cut in on creativity time. Priority was given to what cost us money and not to the talent or brilliance of the campaign. And bit by bit that burden called Frank Wizard started to weigh too much."

"You couldn't get rid of him because you'd created a great company thanks to this character, but in order to keep playing the part you would have had to give up and dump all your dreams."

"That's right, and that's why I went back to The Farm. There I turned back in to Henry Baum. But the important thing was that I went back to being happy with my work."

"And what about your commitment to Oz Company?"

"My commitment could be summed up as continuing to make money for them. Which I did, as the years passed, thanks to the talent of the staff we had in the company. Everything was just set to carry on like that for years, until one day, when you'd already been working for me for some years, you taught me how brilliantly you can shine."

"I don't understand, Henry."

"You were the solution!" His face lit up. "You had everything a person needed to motivate, pick up and perfectly manage a company of this kind. And the experience you needed, well, you'd get it with me until you were ready. Then I started to work it all out.

"The investors would be responsible for their own limited policy. I met Wendy West, an incredible finance manager, and I asked her to play a role: that of a wicked manager who would be concerned only with profits and who would make that everybody's aim above all." He hesitated for a long time. "Believe me, she's a great lady – but in the end she agreed. She realised that the only way to recover the Frank Wizard spirit in the company would be for the company, faced with an enemy like her, to unite and become inspired by a new, fresh, attractive and effective project."

"Mrs. West knew all about it?"

"Yes, Dorothy. Over these past days she, too, has been having a hard time playing her part."

"Now I understand why she visited me the other evening and the messages of encouragement during the meeting," I said in amazement.

"She's a great lady, you'll soon get to know her. But we had to bring the company together again, and the role of a powerful enemy ready to ruin our lives really worked."

"So you worked the whole thing out, then, Henry?" I asked incredulously.

"Don't think ill of me, Freckles, please. All I did was create the opportunity. You've been amazing me more every day, and you really deserve this job. But above all, I realised that with you at the helm, the company would take on all the amazing aspects of your character that you had brought to me. And you've seen that that is how it has been. With that option, you were winning, because you would get the position you really deserve; the workers were winning by gaining a charismatic figure; the colleagues were winning by rediscovering a charismatic personality, by having available to them a person of your talent; and, of course, the company was winning by being able to take advantage of your creativity and your vision for the business. Now is the time for you to enjoy the success you've won."

"Can you imagine what it does to me to hear this?"

"Try to understand me, Freckles. I took what I thought was the right course."

I sat staring into the void, thinking about everything that had happened over those days, assessing my feelings and opportunities, factoring in what it would mean to accept the job, and it was then that I saw everything clearly. I thought for a few moments about the person I was and saw everything.

People tend to remember me because of my hair. It isn't something I'm particularly pleased about, but I have to accept that it's my most noticeable physical feature. The rest of the way I look is what you might call normal. My height is average, my eyes look like everybody else's, even my weight and physical make up are just normal. Every day you'll see hundreds of people who're just like me. To tell the truth, when you look in the mirror in the morning, the person you're looking at looks pretty much like me. That's why I like my hair, and not just because it's long or soft, which it certainly is. I like my hair because that's why people notice me, remember me and take notice of what I have to say at any given moment. It gives power to my words and helps me to get my message across. There's no doubt about it, it's the first thing people see of me, and the last thing they forget about me.

Before I arrived here everybody used to say that I was a nice person, hard working and quite excellent at my work. I was very focussed, and if it should happen that I lost motivation, I could always think of a reason to get right back into the job and concentrate on achieving my goals. But they also use to say that I was too easy going, and sometimes I'd let people get me down. Until today, that is.

Now I'm someone who knows what she wants and knows how to find a way to get it. I'm enthusiastic and exciting. I can motive people, treat them with respect and be demanding, because I'm sensitive to and can take account of their feelings.

My name is Dorothy. I've been living in New York for nearly a year, and today I have taken a decision that is certain to change my whole life and the lives of everyone around me. Today I'm going back to Kansas.

"Henry, I understand that by doing this you thought you would boost the employees' human values, supplied with skills and resources of benefit to the company, and that you would upgrade competitiveness and exigency. By creating an enemy, you were stirring up collaboration between the departments and the working teams. And by giving me this opportunity, you would certainly cause me to develop as a professional and as a person, and that I would reach heights which I never thought I could achieve. Now I am actually a much better person, and I owe it all to you. You know the high esteem I have always held you in and I shall do so for the rest of my life, because I know that there was not one trace of negativity in your decision. But I firmly believe that not everything in the business world is important. I have another model in mind, one you taught me at the Farm.

"I cannot accept the position I have just been offered because I would remember every day when I came to work that I had gained it because of a lie. We should remember that without your help, and the help supplied by Mrs. West, I should never have got it. I should not be able to look my colleagues in the eye without thinking that I'm wearing a mask. There have already been too many characters in the story of this company, too many burdens, too much deception.

"You have suffered vicissitudes which were created by a character. I don't what to transform myself into another character playing a part. I'm excellent, and I know what I will achieve."

"I think I understand…"

"Henry, you know that I believe in the power of people. I believe in development and I firmly believe in optimising personal abilities. I believe in an honest leader, someone who communicates well, someone who is flexible and versatile, a person in whom people can trust."

"But, Freckles, people do trust you," he said in surprise.

"But you must understand that I would always be a deceiver. I can't sustain the structure of my life if the foundation is soft mud. I would have no moral authority to demand confidentiality or commitment to the truth if I were not true to myself."

"But you have the key to success in your hand."

"And I'll get there, but not like this. I want people to recognise my authority and my merits for what I can achieve, not because of fear. I want them to be drawn to my project. If I've done it once, I can do it again."

"What about Oz? I don't want it to fall into the hands of investors who will destroy our dream and the hopes of the staff."

"Don't worry. I understand the intentions which led you to create this whole adventure and I won't leave you in the lurch. Oscar Crow will take the helm of the company as of tomorrow. He has the kind of brain which can create an inspired vision. Tim Mann will be responsible for the staff, and will pay them all the attention they need. His heart is quite big enough for that. And Lionel will defend our image and our hopes in the face of anyone who tries to cast them down. I don't think anybody doubts his courage."

"It might work…"

"Anyway, the investors will carry on relying on Wendy West to provide an image of solvency, seriousness and reliability, although it will help for them to know who she really is. She has already sacrificed too much. It's time she and Heidi buried the hatchet and took their places in a leadership team."

"But what will you do?"

"First, I'm going down to the party to share a drink with you, because I know there are a lot of people there who want to talk to us both. And then I'm going back to Kansas. I'll open my own business and I'll fight to achieve what Frank Wizard achieved. I hope I can count on the help of my wise and trusted friend Henry Baum."

Henry was actually mysteriously sobbing as he smiled hugely at me. After a few moments, looking at me as if he hadn't seen me for years, he answered;

"Never stop shining, Freckles, people like you light up the world."

That night I had a great time at the party. It was my night, and I wasn't going to miss a single second. The peoples' smiles, their hugs, the fantastic encouragement they gave me were the real laurels for our victory. The hours I spent talking with Henry were, as always, educational and a pleasure. It was even a delight to watch him trying to tell one of his stories while the music hammered our eardrums. Tim, Oscar and Lionel watched unbelievingly as Heidi North and Mrs. West chatted about fashion accessories and how Mrs. West thought she was going to melt under the spotlights that lit the meeting. Miss Toto and Boq were seen giggling together in a corner of the bar over endless glasses of champagne and toasting, perhaps for the fourth time, the future of Oz Company.

I had a knot in my stomach as I bade farewell to my friends. I knew I would see them again, but I was amazed at the motivation and support they had given me over those months. They understood the situation perfectly, and promised to fulfil their commitment as though I were doing it myself.

I could always count on them. They were my friends.

Now my never-to-be-forgotten red hair is off on another journey, one which will provide me with endless surprises. Strange clients and fascinating stories. I know that many adventures will occur from now on, that I shall always have the strength to face them, and that I shall never be without another person to motivate me. I have decided to be the mistress of my own destiny and that I deserve to enjoy it every day, and if by some chance it happens that one day I feel a little sad, all I have to do is look in the mirror and I shall be smiling again.

Take hold of the reins of your future and
make your life a fulfilling experience.

BEYOND
THE WRITTEN WORD

Authors who speak to you face to face.

Discover LID Speakers, a service that enables businesses to have direct and interactive contact with the best ideas brought to their own sector by the most outstanding creators of business thinking.

- A network specialising in business speakers, making it easy to find the most suitable candidates.

- A website with full details and videos, so you know exactly who you're hiring.

- A forum packed with ideas and suggestions about the most interesting and cutting-edge issues.

- A place where you can make direct contact with the best in international speakers.

- The only speakers' bureau backed up by the expertise of an established business book publisher.

WHEN GOD WASN'T WATCHING, THE DEVIL CREATED BUSINESS

ISBN: 9781907784001

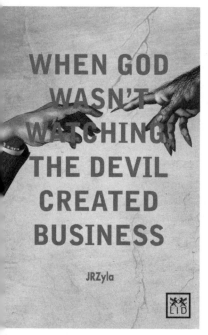

"This will be the cult book for modern executives and managers. Critical, tough and totally inspirational. An absolute eye-opener! You won't be able to put it down because you will feel the significance of the words so strongly."

David Peters, Managing Partner, CEO and Board Practice EMEA, Heidrick & Struggles International.

"This book strips business naked to expose what is good and what is terrible for the human being therein."

Max Landsberg, global bestselling author of *The Tao of Coaching and The Tools of Leadership.*

Does the modern corporate world, especially in times of crisis, resemble what we associate with heaven? Is working in business a heavenly experience or has it increasingly become the opposite? Business people everywhere, not only in executive management, are often working at their physical and emotional limits. It seems the Devil really did have a hand in creating modern business.

This book provides an honest and critical evaluation of our current business philosophies and management values, and looks at what has gone wrong. JRZyla further provides seven practical solutions to help you restore meaning and a higher degree of personal happiness in management and business today.